gURL

W9-AYN-664

THE LOOKS BOOK

A Whole New Approach to Beauty, Body Image, and Style

REBECCA ODES   ESTHER DRILL   HEATHER MCDONALD
ILLUSTRATED BY REBECCA ODES

 PENGUIN BOOKS

A Roundtable Press Book

FOR ROUNDTABLE PRESS, INC.

Directors: **Julie Merberg and Marsha Melnick**

Design: **Georgia Rucker, www.pinkdesigninc.com**

Editor: **Sara Newberry**

Editorial Assistant: **Alison Volk**

Writing and research: **Sue Heinemann and Mikki Halpin**

Style Consultants: **Dan Sharp and Eric Polito**

PENGUIN BOOKS
Published by the Penguin Group
Penguin Putnam Inc.
   375 Hudson Street
   New York, New York, 10014, U.S.A.
Penguin Books Ltd,
   7 Wrights Lane
   London W8 5TZ, England
Penguin Books Australia Ltd
   Ringwood, Victoria, Australia
Penguin Books Canada Ltd
   10 Alcorn Avenue
   Toronto, Ontario, Canada M4V 3B2
Penguin Books(N.Z.) Ltd
   182–190 Wairau Road,
   Auckland 10, New Zealand

Penguin Books Ltd, Registered Offices:
   Harmondsworth, Middlesex, England

10 9 8 7 6 5 4 3 2 1

FOR gURL
Editor-in-Chief: **Esther Drill**
Creative and
   Art Direction: **Rebecca Odes**
   Heather McDonald

CIP data available ISBN 0-14-200211-9

Cover Photograph by Kate Milford
Cover Photo Styling by Dan Sharp

Printed in China

THANK YOU! THANK YOU! THANK YOU!

THE LOOKS BOOK was a huge project and we couldn't have done it alone!

Our sincere thanks to:

Julie Merberg, Sara Newberry, and everyone at Roundtable Press for helping us get it done from start to finish, and to Georgia Rucker for her awesome design skills.

Rhonda Lieberman, for her invaluable input, insight, and archetypal wisdom.

Dan Sharp, for his genius approach to hair, style, and more.

The people whose ideas and expertise made their way into this book via consultation, inspiration or osmosis—and helped to make it better: Mac Chambers, Nicole Childers, Jacob Drill, Rebecca Drill, David Feuer, Sharon Gelman, Mikki Halpin, Tlisza Jaurigue, Craig Kanarick, Kate Milford, Ignazio Moresco, Joan Odes, Naomi Odes, Wendy Olesker, Ian Rogers, Ruth Root, Funke Sangodeyi, Fred Seibert, Daisy Von Furth and the many other friends who have influenced our thoughts on looks, beauty, bodies and style.

The gURLstaff, for their enthusiasm, energy and perseverance!

The girls in the gURL community, for keeping it real and keeping it interesting.

Our families, for constant encouragement and unconditional love.

Craig and Kate, for perspective, patience and support (not to mention craft services and photography).

We love you!

CoNTENTS

PART 1:
A LOOK AT LOOKS...2

PART 2:
THE BODY...32

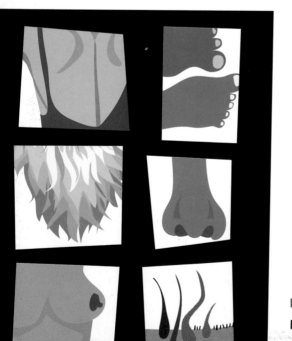

Part 3:
CREATING A LOOK...90

WHY DID WE MAKE THIS BOOK?

We (Esther and Rebecca) have been discussing our looks for a long, long time.

Twenty-something years later at NYU, we met Heather and started **gURL.com** to try to create something that talked about the real stuff girls deal with (rather than focusing on celebrities and models). gURL was a big success, but the best part was hearing what girls really cared about.

A lot of it was about looks.

i'm so hairy!

i'm so bald...

REBECCA

ESTHER

I hate my nose.

My thighs do more than just touch. They overlap.

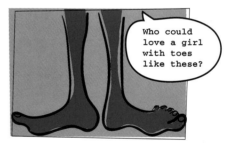

Who could love a girl with toes like these?

We did this book for them, but we also did it for us. When we showed our first book **DEAL WITH IT! A Whole New Approach to Your Body, Brain, and Life as a gURL** to women, the response we heard most often was: "I WISH I HAD THIS BOOK WHEN I WAS GROWING UP!" We felt the same way. We're still dealing with so many issues about how we look and how we feel about it. We wrote this book to explore why looks are such a big deal for us, for girls, for women, and for the whole world... We wanted to show the variety of ways people deal with their looks, and the many possibilities of beauty. When we can get beyond expectations and oppressive ideals and into finding our own style, there's so much opportunity for **power, expression, creativity, experimentation, communication, and plain old FUN!**

WHAT IS **THE LOOKS BOOK?**

It's a three-part investigation into how looks affect our lives—
and how we can take beauty into our own hands.

Part 1 looks at the things that influence how you **think about looks**.
Lots of forces are at work...

Part 2 is about **the body**, your physical presence in the world. Your feelings about
your body are intertwined with your feelings about yourself. You'll find a huge
variety of body attitudes—including how girls and women feel about their own
bodies, part by part (nicknames have been changed for privacy reasons).

Part 3 is a tribute to **style**. Your style is how you present yourself. It's an expression
of how you see the world—and how you want the world to see you. Style gives you
the power to define your own image and become the master of your own beauty
destiny. This is a style sourcebook for ideas and inspiration, packed with timeless
and fabulous looks that go beyond what you see in this month's magazine.

THE LOOKS BOOK is a tool to help you
discover your own ideas about beauty.

We hope you find something in it that
speaks to you...and we hope you enjoy it!

As always, let us know what you think.
www.thelooksbook.com

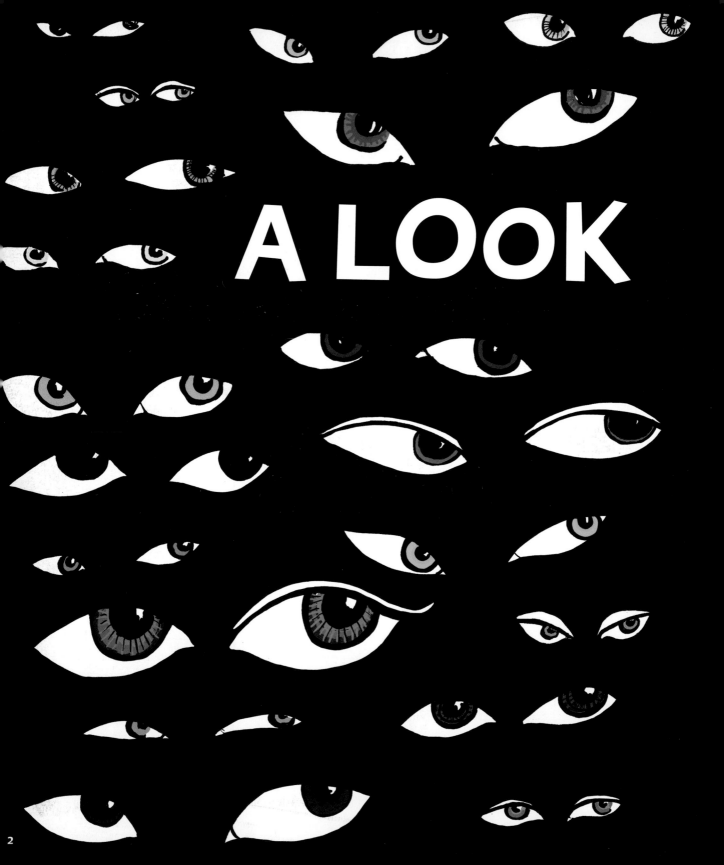

A LOOK

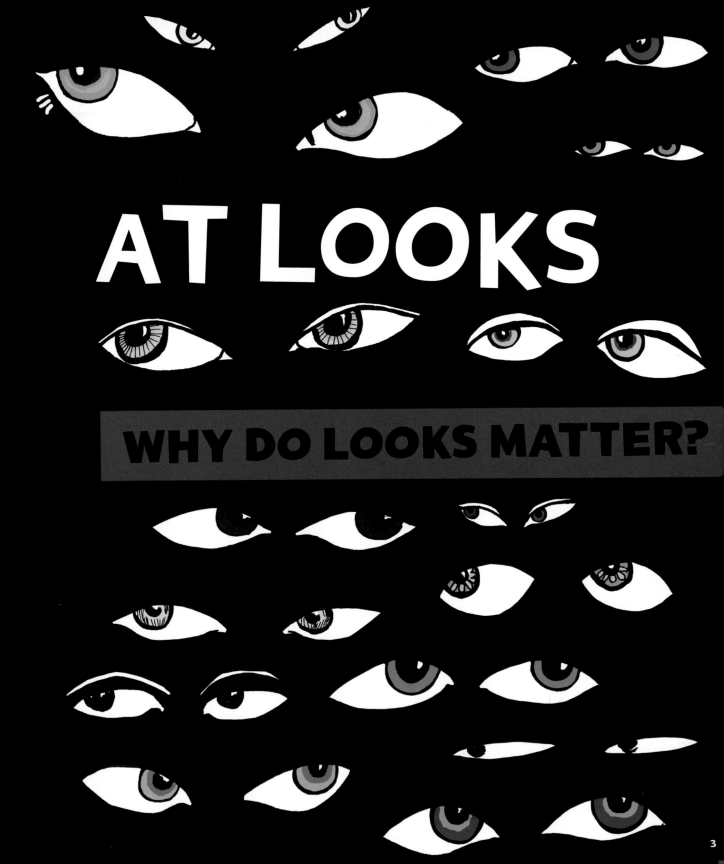

AT LOOKS

WHY DO LOOKS MATTER?

ONE REASON LOOKS MATTER IS **BIOLOGICAL.**

In order to survive, species have to reproduce.
Charles Darwin's famous theory of evolution includes the idea that the way an animal (or plant) looks can help its reproductive cause.

LOOKS CAN HELP TO:

ATTRACT POTENTIAL MATES and
INTIMIDATE THE COMPETITION.

Flowers, with their beautiful, bright colors and alluring scents, are designed to attract the insects that pollinate them, spreading their seeds and helping their species to survive.

At puberty, animals develop traits that distinguish one gender from another. These traits, called secondary sex characteristics, include changes in

SHAPe, COLOR and **ORNAMENTATION.**

They are signs of **fertility**—letting everyone know that the animal is ready and able to reproduce, and is a force to be reckoned with in the competition for mates.

Sometimes the male and female of a species look similar, and their distinguishing characteristics are pretty subtle. When there's a more radical difference between males and females, it's almost always the male who has the obviously alluring characteristics. Many bird species feature elaborate, vibrant male plumage and more low-key coloring for females.

Hey, Big Boy...

Fertility signs are sometimes "presented" to the opposite sex as part of a mating ritual.

This dynamic implies that it's the **male** who's doing the **attracting** and the **female** who's doing the **selecting.**

Scientists think that showy displays like the male peacock's do more than just attract female attention. They can also serve as proof of his genetic **health**—a sick peacock wouldn't have the energy for such a flamboyant presentation.

Humans are animals too.

And we are likely driven by the same urge to reproduce.
So the theory is that we also look for potential mates with traits that indicate

HEALTH and FERTILITY.

VISIBLE SIGNS OF HEALTH INCLUDE:

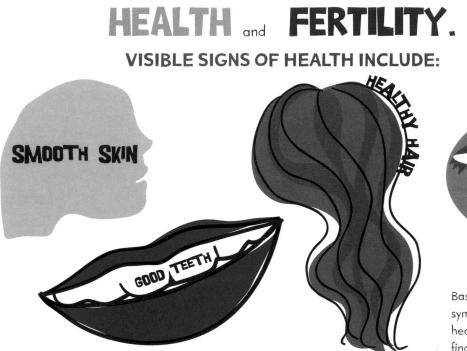

SMOOTH SKIN

GOOD TEETH

HEALTHY HAIR

SYMMETRY

Basic bilateral (left to right) symmetry is associated with health as well as with what we find visually pleasing.

VISIBLE SIGNS OF FERTILITY INCLUDE:

YOUTH
Younger women are more likely to be fertile.

CURVES

Breasts and hips are female secondary sex characteristics that become visible after puberty, at which time people are biologically (but not necessarily mentally!) ready to reproduce. Curves are mostly made of body fat, which is essential for reproduction.

According to the biological theory, **beauty is a reproductive strategy.**
The way we look is designed to attract mates, and to help us sustain our genes and our species. This scientific idea of beauty may help explain why looks matter so much to us.
But the beauty we strive for today goes far beyond the basic need for survival of the species...

WHAT IS BEAUTY?

Beauty is an idea. And everyone's idea of beauty is unique. What you think of as beautiful is shaped by your own life experiences and personal perspectives.

We often think of beauty as what makes us appealing to the people around us, especially potential mates (or dates). But beauty is a function of culture, too—and there are lots of ideas floating around our culture about what is considered beautiful. When **ideas** about beauty make powerful impacts, they can become beauty **ideals**.

What is ideal beauty? Classical Greek philosophers Plato and Aristotle were the first to explore the concept. And our culture is still influenced by this focus on beauty ideals. We see ideal beauty everywhere, from paintings to magazines to TV. The ideals may evolve over time, or they may seem stuck in a permanent loop. Sometimes it can seem like beauty is all about trying to live up to an ideal.

Which is pretty much a hopeless pursuit, because...ideas and ideals aren't real. You are. So, define your own beauty for yourself. Beauty isn't just an idea. It's **your** idea.

JUST AS OUR CULTURE HAS ITS OWN BEAUTY IDEAS AND IDEALS, SO DO OTHER CULTURES. BEAUTY IDEALS IN EVERY CULTURE ARE INFLUENCED BY A MIX OF FACTORS--INCLUDING NATURAL ETHNIC TENDENCIES, MYTHS AND CUSTOMS, AND THE ECONOMIC SITUATION--AND THEY VARY DRAMATICALLY. READ ABOUT HOW SOME NON-WESTERN CULTURES HAVE DEFINED BEAUTY...

A LOT OF WHAT WE KNOW ABOUT BEAUTY THROUGHOUT HISTORY COMES FROM ART.

Our modern images of beauty are seen in movies, magazines, and on TV. But before these modern media existed, painting, sculpture, and early photography were the visual sources for images of beauty.

There's a whole branch of philosophy that examines how beauty is expressed in art. It's called aesthetics.

The word aesthetic also refers to someone's personal idea of what is beautiful.

Even the most "**realistic**" art and media is the product of **choices** made by the artist or media maker.

"REALITY" T.V. IS UNREAL!

These **choices help shape** and are **shaped by** the **beauty ideals** of the culture we live in.

The act of creating an image of beauty can be very powerful. Images can take on lives of their own, transforming one artist's **idea** of beauty into a cultural "**ideal**" of beauty. For this reason, representations of women in art can take on a special status.

So, while images of women in art give us a good idea of what people thought was beautiful at the time, they don't necessarily give us a good idea of what people really looked like.

If I weren't in a *painting,* would you even think I was *pretty?*

Just like magazines and TV today don't really represent an accurate cross section of people in the real world.

ANCIENT BALINESE CARVINGS OF GODDESSES HAVE LONG, HOURGLASS-SHAPED FIGURES WITH SMALL WAISTS...

EARLY IMAGES OF BEAUTY

The earliest images of beauty give us a window into the variety of shapes, sizes, and ways of displaying the body that ancient cultures found beautiful.

The **Venus of Willendorf** (right), the most well-known of all early images of humans, dates from around 24,000 B.C. and was found in Austria. She is admired for her voluptuous form and womanliness. Often, she is interpreted as a goddess of some kind, but her identity is not known. At the very least, she was someone important—everyday women in prehistoric times probably worked too much and ate too little to develop such curves. Whatever she represents, she is a good example of how early beauty ideals focused on rounded body types with overtones of fertility.

Isis and Nefertiti, c. 14th century B.C.

Ancient Egyptian society, which flourished from 3300 to 30 B.C., was a world of complex rituals, and images of women from the era reflect this. In some ways, it seems that the message in Egyptian culture was similar to our own: the ideal of beauty required a great deal of time, effort, and attention to detail. The women of ancient Egypt always appear flawlessly painted and primped.

IN INDIA, 1,000-YEAR-OLD SCULPTURES SHOW VOLUPTUOUS WOMEN WITH FULL BREASTS, BELLIES, AND HIPS...

CLASSICAL BEAUTY

Venus de Milo, c. 150-100 B.C.

Our culture has taken a lot from Ancient Greece and Rome, including many of our words, myths and stories, and even our political system. And we have adopted many of their ideals as well. Ancient Greek philosophers discussed the notion of "ideal beauty." Greco-Roman mythology featured a bevy of gods and goddesses who took on ideal human forms. And classical artists and mathematicians developed systems for determining "ideal" human proportions. The Greek sculptor Polykleitos wrote a book called **The Canon**, which presented the ideal measures and proportions for the human figure. These proportions, primarily based on the principles of symmetry and balance, became the standard of classical beauty in people and in things.

The Greeks developed a geometric formula known as the Golden Mean (known later as the "Divine Proportion" and in the modern era as "Phi"), based on the proportions of humans and other natural creatures, and used this as a basis for designing forms.

Figure measurements based on classical sculpture Venus de Medici

Front View of the Venus de Medici.

Side View of the Venus de Medici.

Back View of the Venus de Medici.

IN 12TH- TO EARLY 20TH-CENTURY CHINA, TINY BOUND FEET WERE AN IMPORTANT PART OF A WOMAN'S BEAUTY...

The Roman engineer Vitruvius further applied these ideal natural proportions to architecture. His texts were interpreted by Leonardo da Vinci, who produced the famous Vitruvian Man drawing to illustrate the perfection of these proportions.

Classical formulas and texts form the seeds of our modern standards of beauty. Many claim that the Golden Mean is the basis of facial attractiveness, and some modern cosmetic surgeons use it to shape "ideal" faces for those who seek them.

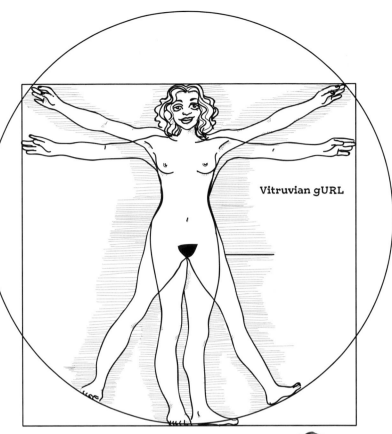

Vitruvian gURL

CALCULATING THE BODY:
the "mathematics" of beauty

There is a theory that the proportion of women's waists to their hips figures in to what we find attractive. Many beauty icons—from voluptuous Marilyn Monroe to svelte Audrey Hepburn—have had close to a 7:10 waist-to-hip ratio (where the waist measures 70% of the hips). However, some studies have shown that people who have not been exposed to Western media do not always prefer this proportion.

In 1932, cosmetic mogul Max Factor developed a Beauty Calibrator that measured the proportions of female faces to determine their "beauty quotient." Based on Hollywood ideals, the device was intended to scout out women with movie-star looks.

Although these mathematical concepts have continued to influence our perceptions of beauty into the modern era, lots of other ideals have been expressed through art and media throughout history...

A QUICK LOOK at BEAUTY IN ^WESTERN ART

Sandro Botticelli
The Birth of Venus
1482

Botticelli's women, with gentle curves and serene faces, are still among the most powerful images of beauty in art. Even today, a woman with flowing curls and an ethereal look is described as having a Botticelli beauty.

Lucas Cranach the Elder
Cupid Complaining to Venus
c. 1530s

In the 15th and early 16th centuries, the ideal body was S-shaped, with a sway back, small, high breasts, and a rounded, protruding stomach, as well as large feet. Most images of women from the early Renaissance feature significant bellies, implying that fertility was seen as beautiful in a literal way.

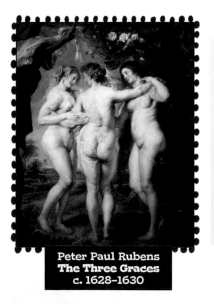

Peter Paul Rubens
The Three Graces
c. 1628–1630

Rubens was the master of late Northern Renaissance painting. His nudes (and other nudes of the era) glorified the beauty of flesh and softness, showing women with curves, dimples, rolls, and even cellulite. These traits were considered marks of beauty at the time. The term "Rubenesque" is still used to describe a voluptuous kind of beauty.

IN AFRICA, 18TH-CENTURY MENDE MASKS FROM SIERRA LEONE SHOW ROLLS OF FAT AROUND THE NECK...

Éduoard Manet
Olympia
1863

Paul Gauguin
Two Tahitian Women
1899

The reclining nude has been a popular subject throughout art history, and the way artists chose to represent these lounging ladies gives us lots of insight into beauty ideals across the centuries. Nudes were historically painted in mythological or biblical scenes.

People found this painting shocking when it was first shown in Paris because of the woman's direct gaze, as well as her modern accessories. Earlier reclining nudes had been cloaked in mythical mystery, never confronting the viewer. Manet portrayed his model as a real naked person rather than a fantasy nude.

Post-Impressionist painter Paul Gauguin was one of the first major European artists to glorify non-European beauty. When he moved to the South Pacific in the 1890s, he created masterpieces featuring the women whose looks were so different from those he had seen at home. Other artists working around the turn of the century, including Pablo Picasso and Gustav Klimt, were similarly inspired by African, Asian, and other foreign imagery and subjects—and helped broaden the definition of beauty.

René Magritte
The Rape
1934

The growth of photography pushed painting away from realism and into the abstract. Surrealism created a new way of seeing the world, and envisioned the body in fantastical ways loaded with innuendo.

This surrealist painting shows how the body and sexuality are made public by the viewer's imagination—it's the ultimate expression of being "undressed" by someone's eyes.

Surreal and abstract views of the body opened up the idea of beauty beyond the literal and had a huge impact on the modern aesthetic.

Cindy Sherman
Untitled 183
from the "History"
series 1989-1990

In the modern era, women are known as artists instead of just subjects. Photographer Cindy Sherman is both— her artwork explores how women have been represented in art and media, using herself as a model. These redesigned images make us think about how representations of women affect how we see beauty, in art and in ourselves.

IN 19TH-CENTURY HAWAII, A 6-FOOT-TALL, 300-POUND RULER WAS KNOWN FOR HER BEAUTY AS WELL AS HER POWER...

13

beauty and CELEBRITY

The invention of photography had a huge influence on 20th-century images of beauty. While photography appears to mirror reality, it has rarely been "realistic." Photographers discovered early on that by manipulating the light, exposure, and other factors in an image, they could create something that was more like art than a document of reality.

Motion pictures became big business in the early part of the 20th century. And the industry's most famous products—its actresses and actors—came out of the studios' star system. Movie studios thoroughly shaped their stars' images, often transforming an actress's identity, through fashion and publicity spin, into something the studio considered more attractive to the public.

Joan Crawford before

Joan Crawford after

Publicity photos were glamorous, highly posed, and stylized. Each was the product of a complex process involving a team of people—photographer, makeup artist, hair and clothing stylists, lighting experts, et cetera—all doing their best to create the right effect.

After the film was developed it was often retouched to perfect the image. The same extensive beautification process applies to most photos we see in fashion magazines today. Digital technology has made it even easier to alter photographs realistically, erasing "imperfections" and changing proportions.

Movies were an important trend-setting medium. Looking at images of Hollywood beauties, women in America began to copy their glamorous looks. Louise Brooks and Clara Bow (the "It" girl) modeled the Flapper look that swept the U.S. in the 20s. And in 1931, Jean Harlow's platinum blonde hair (showcased in the movie "Platinum Blonde") created a bleaching frenzy. Hundreds of other styles and trends were sparked by the hairstyles and fashions worn by celebrities in movies and on the pages of magazines.

SEE THE FLAPPER PAGE 112

Jean Harlow

Anna Mae Wong

By the turn of the 20th century, advances in communication, travel and commerce had opened the U.S. and Europe up to the rest of the world; art and media felt strong influences from non-Western cultures. Striking performances in Paris and New York by the Ballets Russes, an avant-garde Russian dance group, sparked a new interest in looks inspired by Asia, Africa and the Middle East. In the 20s and 30s, these looks were personified on-screen by ethnic beauties like Anna Mae Wong, Theda Bara, and Pola Negri, and offscreen by stars like Josephine Baker, who captured the public's imagination. Their roles played on the stereotype of the other as "exotic"—mysterious, foreign, and often sexualized. For all of its typecasting, this was the most multicultural moment in Hollywood history until the late 20th century.

THE BANGWA AND OTHER TRIBES IN WEST AFRICA VIEW FATNESS AS AN ESSENTIAL ELEMENT OF BEAUTY...

Madonna, 1985

By mid-century, when almost every family had a TV in their living room, new celebrities were born every day. Television also provided access to the look (and moves) of musicians—from "Elvis the Pelvis" to Madonna and beyond. The unique looks and styles of pop, hip-hop, and other music stars have had a major impact on our culture's beauty image, especially for young people.

Madonna wanna-bes

FOR MORE ON MUSIC AND STYLE, SEE PAGE 146

The modern era has spawned a kind of celebrity whose whole reason for being famous is her looks—the supermodel. Women have been fashion models since the first couture shows at the beginning of the 20th century, and models became stars in their own right in the 50s. More than just a fashion model, the supermodel is an icon so gorgeous that everybody knows her name. (Beauty pageants, though they profess to choose winners based on more than just looks, create another kind of beauty-based celebrity.) While supermodel culture peaked in the 1980s, it continues to churn out new faces and figures to define the beauty ideal of the moment.

Naomi Campbell, Elle MacPherson, and Claudia Schiffer

PIN-UPS AND CENTERFOLDS

Pin-ups, mass-produced images of women (or men) in flirty, provocative poses, have been around for a long time. Images of nudes in Renaissance paintings were supposedly copied by artisans and purchased by men. Sexy women have been popular subjects since the time photography was invented. The first magazines made especially for men were published during World War I. But the real revolution in "girlie" magazines, as they were called, was the launch of Playboy in 1953. This was the first mainstream magazine to feature photographs of nude women (Marilyn Monroe appeared in the premier issue).

Pamela Anderson

Men's magazines, as well as more explicit pornographic magazines, feature images that are designed to appeal to men in a sexual way. As a result, the women in these magazines have generally been curvaceous and sultry, while women's magazines promoted a "clothes hanger" look. Recently, however, the gap between Playboy centerfolds and fashion models has been narrowing. The widespread use of plastic surgery has allowed women of all shapes to acquire the large breasts favored by men's magazines. Some of today's pop stars don't look much different than yesterday's porn stars. As our society becomes more comfortable with sexuality and nudity, images once considered pornographic become acceptable and even beautiful.

BEFORE MARRIAGE, BANGWA WOMEN ARE SENT TO A "FATTENING HOUSE" WHERE THEY EAT ENRICHED FOODS...

MONEY, POWER and BEAUTY

They're just.... breathtaking.

stunning.

$ $ $ $

Another major factor that has influenced our idea of beauty is MONEY.

In our society, money is power. And power has always played a part in what the culture defines as beautiful and desirable. Historically, looks that implied wealth and status were equated with beauty and looks that were identified with working-class or poor people were thought to be less beautiful.

The interesting thing is that as society evolved, so did the physical traits associated with richness and poorness. This sometimes resulted in a total turnaround of beauty ideals.

Until about 80 years ago in **E**urope and the U.S., rich people kept their skin as white as possible—because they could. A wealthy person would carry a parasol, wear a wide-brimmed hat, or just stay indoors to protect her creamy complexion. Skin that was tanned and weathered was associated with menial outdoor work. By the 1920s, with more people spending their workdays indoors, pallor started to signify being trapped in an office all day. Rich people began taking beach vacations, making a suntan the mark of the lady of leisure. The "healthy" suntanned look has remained something of an ideal, even though it's been determined that tanning is actually hazardous to the health and damaging to the appearance. "Self-tanning" products aim to reconcile this look with our knowledge of the negative consequences.

FOR MORE ON SUN AND SKIN CARE, SEE PAGE 76

A recent study of girls in Fiji shows the impact of Western beauty ideals on non-Western cultures. Fiji, a remote island nation in the Pacific, has always promoted a well-fed, robust physique as a sign of health and prosperity. Thin bodies were considered sickly—weight loss was cause for concern. After American television was introduced to Fiji in 1995, images of Hollywood-thin TV stars triggered an outbreak of dieting, self-esteem problems, and eating disorders among teenage girls.

FOR THE NIGERIAN YORUBA, WHO DECORATE THEIR BODIES WITH SCARS, BEAUTY IS TIED TO COURAGE AND ENDURING PAIN...

SIZE AND STATUS

Economic conditions have also triggered dramatic changes in the idealized body shape. Historically, when food and money were hard to come by, larger (well-fed) body types were more idealized. Along these same lines, times of plenty traditionally correlated with thinner body ideals. Whenever there has been food to go around, the wealthy person asserted her status by her ability to spend time and money keeping herself fit. This model is sustained today in most developed countries, although there are many cultures (and lots of people!) who hold bountiful bodies in esteem.

Sometimes it wasn't the aristocrats who set the trends. In 15th- and 16th-century Europe, sumptuary laws were passed to restrict anyone but the upper classes from wearing certain clothes. Commoners were forbidden to wear luxurious fabrics and, in some cases, more than one color. Merchants, who had plenty of money to spend on clothes but were subject to these restrictions, came up with a creative form of rebellion—they began slashing their clothes to reveal other rich, colorful fabrics underneath. Ironically, this look became wildly popular with the aristocrats who had created the restrictive laws that brought it about.

FOR MORE ON BOTTOM-UP FASHION, SEE STREET STYLE, PAGE 144

THE RADICALLY DIFFERENT IDEAS OF BEAUTY MAINTAINED BY DIFFERENT CULTURES FLOW FROM UNIQUE CULTURAL TRADITIONS, AS WELL AS FROM THE WAY THAT SOME BODY PARTS NATURALLY DIFFER BY ETHNICITY: SLANTED ASIAN EYES, DARK AFRICAN SKIN, BLONDE SCANDINAVIAN HAIR, AND SO ON.

THE U.S. IS THE MOST CULTURALLY AND ETHNICALLY DIVERSE COUNTRY IN THE WORLD. EVEN SO, THERE HAS HISTORICALLY BEEN A DOMINANT CULTURAL AESTHETIC THAT IDEALIZES PEOPLE OF EUROPEAN DESCENT. THIS SITUATION CAN HAVE A HUGE EFFECT ON NON-EUROPEAN PEOPLE, WHO OFTEN FIND THEMSELVES IDEALIZING THE DOMINANT AESTHETIC. IN MUCH OF THE AFRICAN-AMERICAN COMMUNITY, FOR EXAMPLE, THE STRAIGHT-HAIRED, LIGHT-SKINNED IDEAL RULED FOR MOST OF THE 20TH CENTURY. THE MISS BRONZE AMERICA BEAUTY CONTEST, STARTED IN 1927, TENDED TO CROWN WINNERS OF THIS MOLD, AND THERE WAS A TREMENDOUS MARKET FOR SKIN BLEACHERS AND HAIR RELAXERS. AFTER WORLD WAR II, EYELID JOBS TO "WESTERNIZE" ASIAN EYES BY CREATING A DOUBLE FOLD BECAME MORE WIDESPREAD. THE INCREASINGLY MULTI-CULTURAL MAKEUP OF OUR COUNTRY HAS CHANGED THIS DYNAMIC, AND WILL CONTINUE TO EXPAND THE DEFINITION OF WHAT IS BEAUTIFUL.

BEAUTY IS IN THE 👁 OF THE BEHOLDER.

NATURE, CULTURE, MEDIA AND MONEY ALL CONTRIBUTE TO OUR IDEA OF WHAT IS BEAUTIFUL—BUT THEY DON'T DEFINE IT. IN THE END, BEAUTY IS SUBJECTIVE, AND ONLY THE INDIVIDUAL CAN DECIDE WHAT HE OR SHE FINDS BEAUTIFUL.

What you see is defined by who you are. Whether you're looking at a person or a painting, no one else will ever have the exact same view of something as you do.

That's because no two people have the same brain or the same experiences. Your ideas and ideals are affected by your personal perspective.

Your identity and psychology impact how you see everything, especially people.

PURR. PHOOEY.

POSITIVE ASSOCIATIONS AND FAMILIAR TIES CAN LEAD TO IDEAS OF BEAUTY.

hot!

FAVORITE AUNT'S WEDDING PICTURES

reminds him of

NEGATIVE ASSOCIATIONS CAN AFFECT BEAUTY IDEALS AS WELL.

not.

NASTY GEOMETRY TEACHER

reminds him of

SELF	OTHER
☺	☀
(boring)	(fascinating)

THE ATTRACTION OF DIFFERENCE CAN ALSO MAKE A POWERFUL IMPACT ON BEAUTY.

JOLIE/LAIDE

Beauty that falls outside the ideal has its own appeal. **Jolie laide** (also called **belle laide**) is a French term which literally means "pretty ugly." It's used to describe a woman whose looks are so distinctive that she could fall into either category, depending on any number of factors—her mood, the light, and who's doing the looking. In fact, almost everyone's beauty is affected by other people's feelings about them. Have you ever thought someone was gorgeous until something in her behavior made you look at her in a different way?

The beauty ideals of society as a whole don't always correspond directly to the beauty ideals of individuals. At any given time in history, no matter what the ideal woman looked like, there were thousands and thousands of people who preferred her opposite.

So whether or not you share the traits of the so-called beauty of the moment, it's likely that your kind of beauty will mesh with someone else's idea of beautiful.

The point is, **BEAUTY** is however you see it, which is, in effect:

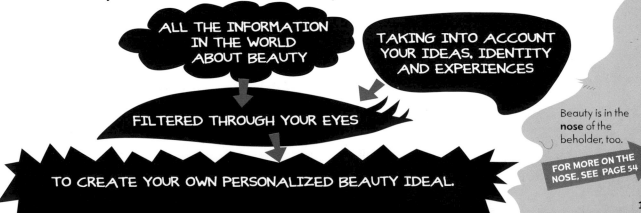

ALL THE INFORMATION IN THE WORLD ABOUT BEAUTY

TAKING INTO ACCOUNT YOUR IDEAS, IDENTITY AND EXPERIENCES

FILTERED THROUGH YOUR EYES

Beauty is in the **nose** of the beholder, too.

FOR MORE ON THE NOSE, SEE PAGE 54

TO CREATE YOUR OWN PERSONALIZED BEAUTY IDEAL.

BEAUTIFUL?

Unless you miraculously happen to match the ideal of the moment, modern beauty requires a certain amount of primping, plucking, and numerous other processes. Although the methods change and the ideals vary, people have always worked at being beautiful. Decorating, dressing, and even molding their bodies to fit the beauty model, women dedicate enormous amounts of resources to the quest for beauty—sometimes endangering themselves in the process.

Fashion is a big part of beauty. The shifting shapes and silhouettes reflect the roller coaster of historical beauty ideals.

The ability to pursue fashion and beauty is related to wealth and leisure. In ancient times, fashion was only for the upper class, people who actually had the money and time to spend on beauty routines. As fashions and products became more widely distributed, less wealthy people were able to acquire the trappings of beauty as well, and began to influence the beauty ideal.

FOR INFO ON THE DIFFERENT WAYS WOMEN AROUND THE WORLD HAVE PURSUED BEAUTY WITH HAIRSTYLES, MAKEUP AND SKINCARE RITUALS, SEE PAGES 50, 85 AND 77.

In ancient Egypt (starting around 3300 B.C.), people of all classes bathed daily, anointed themselves with perfumed oils, and wore tattoos, jewelry, and distinctive dark eye make-up. Women wore elaborately braided wigs and hair extensions (sometimes over shaved heads).

From the 5th to the 4th century B.C., Greek women and slaves made their families' robes out of long rectangular strips of fabric that were elaborately draped, with tucks, pleats, and folds to keep the material in place. Details such as braiding, belts and shoulder pins were common features of the women's robes, which were often decorated to represent the wearer's city-state.

Elizabethan fashion (in 15th-century England) was meant to convey power and luxury while downplaying femininity—the triangular bodice shielded curves and looked like armor. Queen Elizabeth I was the prime trendsetter of the time, creating a craze for strawberry blonde hair and pale skin. Most aristocratic women used white paint to create a pale face, and some drew bluish veins on their skin for a translucent effect. These paints damaged the skin, and sometimes more.

Created by illustrator Charles Dana Gibson at the end of the 19th century, the Gibson Girl represented a new, modern, sporty American ideal of beauty and style. Her outfits started a trend for fitted, embroidered shirts and long, tapered skirts. Underneath it all, she wore the S-curve corset, swaying her back and pushing her chest foward into a "monobosom." The Gibson Girl look influenced 20 years of style.

Early 20th-century Western fashion reflected an increasing interest in non-Western cultures. This translated to draped, columnar styles that seemed to have more in common with togas, kimonos and Turkish harem pants than the corseted figures that came before them. Patterns and fabrics had an Asian or Middle Eastern feel.

Christian Dior launched the "New Look" in 1947, promising a rebirth of fashion and femininity after the modest and serious World War II era. The cinched waist and full skirt forced a return to corsetry and spawned the 1950s poodle skirt look. Dior's shoe designer came up with the steel-spiked, super-narrow needle heel—aka the stiletto.

Pre-revolutionary (mid-18th century) France was all about excess, and marked the introduction of the "wedding cake" dress. Enormous volume was created by layers upon layers of hoops and petticoats, sometimes making dresses so puffy that the wearer was unable to fit through entryways. Hairstyles were high and elaborate, too. When smallpox ravaged the population (and their complexions) in the 17th century, people wore spots of colored cloth to cover the disfiguring scars left by the disease. This fashion evolved into painted-on "beauty marks."

In the beginning of the 19th century in Europe and the U.S., high-waisted dresses were popular. Worn without corsets, this look was influenced by the drapery of classical Greece and Rome. Today, the empire waist is still popular in evening wear, as well as in baby-doll dresses.

The 1960s saw a revolution in women's fashion. Women were looking for comfort and fun in their clothes. This era marked the beginning of widespread college attendance by women, and casual clothes to match. While pants had been worn by some daring style mavens (and women of the work force) since around 1920, it wasn't until the 1960s that it started to become acceptable for grown women to wear pants in public.

Disco style dominated the mainstream in the late 70s and early 80s. Disco fashion made everyone into a showgirl—the whole idea was to wear something that would make you stand out on a dance floor full of other shiny, sparkly people. Attention-getting hairdos like afros and wings were also popular. Partygoers and glitter-lovers everywhere are still fans of disco style today.

In the 1980s, the Dress For Success aesthetic created a uniform of acceptable officewear, de rigueur for anyone who hoped to climb the corporate ladder. Women in the workplace wore "Power Suits" with strong lines and exaggerated shoulder pads. Big hair was also in style, adding to the commanding appearance of the 80s success-dresser.

RITUAL DRESS

Rituals are ceremonies that mark rites of passage, religious events or celebrations—and the clothing we wear to these rituals helps to define them as special.

The institution of marriage is usually marked with a ceremony (often religious) and celebration. The dress of brides around the world reflects the very different ideas cultures have about what defines beauty—from the pristine American Judeo-Christian bride in "virginal" white to the **mendhi**-decorated Hindu bride in red and gold glory.

AMERICAN BRIDE

HINDU BRIDE

Color is a significant part of ritual dress, and means different things in different cultures. In India, white is the ritual color of mourning and red is the color of celebration. But in the United States, black is the color of mourning and white symbolizes purity.

The women of the Maasai tribes in Africa are famous for their elaborate beaded jewelry in red, orange, white, green, and blue. During the two most important ceremonies in a Maasai girl's life (coming of age and marriage), she shaves her head, and wears handmade beaded necklaces, bracelets, and earrings.

Rituals and dress are important parts of cultural identity and often help maintain traditions and cultural integrity. When one culture dominates another, traditions of ritual and dress are often lost. In the United States, the aesthetic (as well as the guns) of the dominant culture took a large toll on the Native American population and culture. Native Americans carry on the customs of their culture by wearing traditional regalia at private and public rituals.

MAASAI TRIBESWOMAN

OJIBWA INDIAN c 1900

DICTATED DRESS

Dress can be dictated by any authority—a school, a corporation, a religion.

Many uniforms serve to identify people as belonging to a specific group, from a sports team to a branch of the military. Schools sometimes institute uniforms to create a sense of equality in dress and to enforce modesty. Dress codes are a milder version of the same impulse.

Religious dress distinguishes the wearer and the group from the general public. Some religions, especially in their orthodox or fundamentalist forms, have laws about modesty, often aimed at preventing a woman from being perceived in a sexual manner by men other than her husband. The belief behind these restrictions is that men are unable to control their natural urges, so the onus is on the woman to make herself unattractive or invisible. The Islamic **hijab** (which comes from the Arabic word "to conceal") requires that a woman be covered in loose fabric, exposing no more than her face and hands. The fundamentalist Islamic Taliban regime in Afghanistan (1996–2001) took this to an extreme in the sometimes violent enforcement of the wearing of the **burqa**, which covered a woman's entire face and body.

MOROCCAN ISLAMIC HIJAB

Secular ideologies can define rules of style as well. The communist Chinese Cultural Revolution of the 1960s (led by Chairman Mao) made traditional Chinese clothing and western styles unacceptable. Instead, the military uniform—a blue cotton Mao jacket, with its stand-up collar, and loose pants—became popular for men and women. The traditional Chinese **cheongsam**, a sheath dress with side slits and mandarin collar, was seen as a symbol of pre-Communist China, and was therefore unpopular with staunch party supporters. Women wearing cheongsams were harassed and even prosecuted. In 1978, when China established its Open Door Policy to the rest of the world, individuality in dressing was finally accepted again.

MAOIST "UNIFORM"

EXTREMES of BEAUTY

The **corset** is a device used to shape the torso dating back to the 14th century. Made of materials such as whalebone, iron, and steel, corsets whittled the waist, and often enhanced the breasts and hips.

Corset shapes evolved over time. In the 1800s, the corset was at its most damaging. Laces in back were tied super-tight to create a tiny 18-inch or smaller waist. The corset was definitely an upper-class garment—it restricted movement and required a maid to lace it.

Worn continuously, corsets actually changed the body. Many young girls were outfitted with corsets as a way of straightening their posture and "training" their waists, sometimes starting in infancy. As a result, muscles that normally hold the body upright didn't get a chance to develop and so corsets actually became a body-support necessity. A few women, desiring extra-tiny waists, had a lower rib removed so they could pull the stays even tighter.

In the late 1800s, despite warnings that corsets were causing fainting spells and other health complaints, they got even tighter in an effort to mold the fashionable S-shaped figure. The bicycle craze of the 1890s helped to stop the madness. Riding a bicycle in a corset was asking for an accident; plus, the beauty ideal began to shift to a more healthy-looking, vigorous woman.

Corsets are still worn today under structured eveningwear and even as slightly out-there outerwear. The modern corset can have some sexual connotations and is often featured in lingerie photo shoots.

High heels have been fashionable since the 1600s, when both men and women wore them. In the 1750s, aristocratic French women donned 4-inch Pompadour heels, named after the king's mistress. Revolutionary, anti-aristocratic sentiment kicked high heels out of fashion at the end of the 18th century. But they made a comeback in the late 1860s—and heels have gone up and down ever since.

Many people associate high heels with sexiness. This is largely because they change the shape of the body, tensing the legs and thrusting out the boobs and butt for balance. The walk changes too, emphasizing the sway of the hips. But high heels can be painful to wear; wearing them regularly can result in back pain, shortened leg muscles, and other foot discomforts.

Throughout history, women (and men) have repeatedly placed their bodies in harm's way to try to achieve the beauty ideals of the day.

ALSO SEE PERMANENT ALTERATIONS OF THE BODY, PAGE 88

Poisonous cosmetics

In countries all around the world, there is a long history of people putting themselves in danger to change the color of their skin. In the 1600s, European men and women applied ceruse—a poisonous combination of vinegar, egg whites, and lead—to their faces, necks, shoulders, and chests to get the high-status pale complexion. Lead remained a key ingredient in skin-lightening cosmetics until the end of the 19th century, when medical journals began to report a growing number of serious cases of lead poisoning. In the Carribean and in some African countries, skin lightening creams known to be poisonous are still used today.

A variety of other cosmetics were also found to be dangerous. Fucus, a red lip balm popular in the 16th century, contained the poison mercuric sulfide. At the same time, belladonna, which was added to the eyes to make them brighter and widen the pupils, severely damaged the eyes. In 1938, the U.S. Congress finally passed the Food, Drug and Cosmetic Act, which outlawed some of the more toxic ingredients in use, after two books—**100,000 Guinea Pigs** (1933) and **American Chamber of Horrors** (1938)—revealed just how unsafe a lot of beauty products were. Even today, however, we use beauty products with ingredients thought to be toxic.

R.I.P.
Lady anne
GAVE HER
LIFE FOR A
PEACHES AND
CREAM
COMPLEXION

There is a strong message in our society about the power of beauty.

The idea of a woman's beauty granting her power (over men, usually) is a common theme in our media and myths. It shows up in biblical texts as well, from Adam and Eve to Samson and Delilah. The barrage of images of ideal beauty we see every day reinforces the idea that powerful things happen to beautiful women. The result: huge amounts of time, energy, and money spent in pursuit of beauty.

Although the obsession may be real, the power of beauty is limited and ephemeral. And plenty of women achieve power in our society outside the narrow box of current beauty ideals.

ALL THIS?

The truth is that beauty does not lead to happiness. But there is a lot invested in keeping us worried about how we look. Beauty and fashion are major, billion-dollar industries—the more people worry, the more they spend on things that might make them look "better." Our concern often continues as we get older, not surprising given how many of our images of beauty are tied to youth.

Understanding the forces at work can give us perspective—but doesn't mean we have to feel bad about wanting to be beautiful. So enjoy (and endure) as many purchases, processes, and procedures as you please. The important thing is to maintain your own ideal of beauty from your own unique perspective, not to chase an ideal that is by its very definition elusive.

BEAUTY IS A BUSINESS.

The beauty business and the fashion business are separate entities with a lot of overlap and a common purpose: to make money from selling people the idea of beauty. Both the fashion and beauty industries took off around the turn of the 20th century. Until then, cosmetics, seen as health and beauty aids, were mostly a matter of folklore and recipe books.

In the beginning, the beauty industry was really built by women. A number of early **beauty entrepreneurs** were immigrant or African-American women, who made millions producing and distributing beauty products. Annie Turnbo Malone and Madame C.J. Walker became millionaires developing products for black hair and skin. Helena Rubenstein and Elizabeth Arden both immigrated to the U.S. and remade themselves as American beauty moguls. The tradition continues today as women create and market innovative beauty products.

Fashion designers are among the most influential creative forces in our culture, generating fashions that inspire powerful trends. Some designers are elevated to cult status, either through their clothing or their own eccentric personalities. Coco Chanel was the first genuine "celebrity" designer. Designers have the unique opportunity to create fashion, drawing inspiration from history, the street, or wherever they find it.

THE MYTH OF THE MUST-HAVE

When the idea of beauty changes, as when something goes in and out of style, it creates demand for products that create the new look. With the assistance of fashion magazines, the fashion industry specializes in developing powerful objects of desire and a sense of the must-have item.

> A SIX MONTH WAIT FOR THE STRAPPY SANDALS ON PAGE 103? BUT THEY'LL BE TOTALLY OVER BY THEN!

KEEPING SUPPLIES **LIMITED** ENSURES THAT DEMAND FOR THE **MUST-HAVES** STAYS HIGH.

It's easy (and sometimes really fun) to get sucked in to the world of the must-haves. But considering how hard they are to find and afford, it can be useful to think about whether it's worth shelling out all that time and money. The hysterical "need" for a certain brand of jeans or pair of shoes is about more than the product itself. It's about marketing desire.

THE CYCLE OF FASHION

TAKE, FOR EXAMPLE, BELL-BOTTOMS
(ORIGINALLY SEEN ON SAILORS)

HIPPIE ANTI-ESTABLISHMENT FASHION IN THE LATE 1960S

FASHION DESIGNERS GET INSPIRED... MAGAZINES FOLLOW SUIT

BECOME MAINSTREAM IN MID 1970S

MEANWHILE... PUNK CULTURE EMERGES IN LATE 1970S WITH SKINNY PANTS

FASHION DESIGNERS GET INSPIRED...

BELL-BOTTOMS GO "OUT" AND END UP IN THRIFT STORES

WHERE THEY SIT, UNTIL...

HIPSTERS IN THE EARLY 1990S GO **THRIFTING** AND BUY BELL-BOTTOMS... RAVERS WEAR WIDE-LEG BELLS

FASHION DESIGNERS GET INSPIRED... MAGAZINES FOLLOW SUIT

BECOME **MAINSTREAM** IN THE LATE 1990S

Magazines for women originated in France in the 18th century, and have been influencing women ever since. Showing women what to wear and how to stay in tune with the times, the magazines also featured ads for "miracle creams" and other cosmetic products promising to transform the buyer's appearance.

The modern age of women's magazines was sparked in part by a need for beauty manufacturers to publicize their products.

ADVERTISING CREATES THE ILLUSION THAT A PRODUCT WILL BRING YOU CLOSER TO THE CURRENT IDEAL.

In the early 1950s, cosmetics advertising began to play up the sexiness of makeup with Revlon's phenomenally successful campaign for its "Fire and Ice" line of red lipstick and nail polish. In two years, from 1950 to 1952, cosmetics annual sales jumped from $400 million to over a billion.

This relationship between promotion and editorial integrity has plagued women's magazines since their early days—one famous French beauty magazine was actually created by the president of L'Oréal in the 1930s as a vehicle to write about L'Oréal products.

Even today, there are strong ties between sponsors and magazines—magazines are supported by advertisers of fashion and beauty products, and are interested in keeping them happy.

Women's magazines are the mouthpiece of the fashion and beauty industry. They are how women find out about the latest styles and trends, distilled from high-fashion couture and repackaged for the average woman.

Models are the public faces of the fashion and beauty businesses. Fashion models look the way they do because they make clothes look better: basically, a skinnier body is less likely to interfere with the lines of a high-fashion garment. Models are human clothes-hangers, canvasses for designers and styling crews. While a girl with "character" will occasionally rise to the top, more often what people look for in a model is a blank slate that can be easily transformed into a multitude of looks—a clean surface to project their fantasies onto. Our culture is fixated on models. The extreme physique and picturesque face required for success in the modeling industry are difficult to come by—part of the allure of models is their "freak of nature" quality.

In most cases, being a model means being:

1. under 20
2. exceptionally close to the ideal for facial beauty
3. in the top 10% of height
4. in the bottom 2% of weight
5. in the right place at the right time

Despite the fact that very few women share these traits, many young women dream of becoming models. It is unfortunate that the most desired career for many girls is one that can be achieved by so few, and is only focused on physical appearance. There are so many great things to be that allow a girl to control her own destiny, rather than allow it to be determined by the size of her body or the shape of her face.

OWN YOUR OWN LOOK!

Of course you're concerned about your looks.
It's natural...and it's part of being human.

So, what do you do if you don't happen to look exactly like
a supermodel or a pop star or the beauty icon of the moment?

You have a choice.
You can spend a lot of money and a lot of energy trying to
achieve the elusive ideal or you can find your own ideal.

People throughout history and around the world have found
so many different kinds of bodies and styles beautiful. Choose
an ideal that works for you (or make one up). IF SOMEONE
DOESN'T LIKE IT, YOU CAN BET THERE'S
SOMEONE ELSE OUT THERE WHO WILL.

Amidst all the forces to contend with
and ideals to compare yourself to,
remember the most important force
and ideal of all: YOU.

Beauty is about how you express yourself—
your looks, your image, your personality.

A common ingredient in every beauty ideal is **self-confidence.**

THE KIND OF BEAUTY THAT REALLY KNOCKS PEOPLE'S SOCKS OFF, OR MAKES THEM SMILE WHEN THEY SEE YOU, IS THE KIND THAT COMES FROM INSIDE...

the kind that comes from someone who is in control of her own destiny.

Your beauty is YOUR OWN.

So the next time you look in the mirror and your brain gets flooded with those inevitable unflattering thoughts and comparisons and general badness, try to take a step back and acknowledge the whole crazy world of beauty and looks obsession that makes you think that way. And then...maybe you'll see that you have the power to create your own look.

Have fun with it.

Take matters into your own hands.

Experiment. Experience. Enjoy.

Make your own beauty.

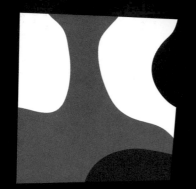

THE

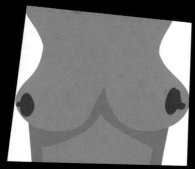

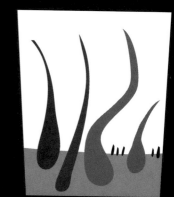

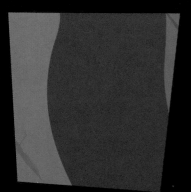

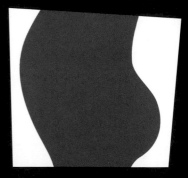

BODY

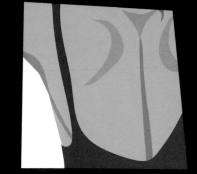

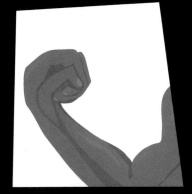

BODY IMAGE

Your body image is your own idea of what your body looks like. The way people feel about themselves has a huge impact on the way they feel about their bodies—and the way people feel about their bodies has a huge impact on the way they feel about themselves in general. Body image is often connected to self-esteem, self-confidence, and self-worth.

When it comes to our bodies, we've all got our own unique set of raw materials that we're born with, created by our genes (and the genes of our parents, our parents' parents, and so on). And everyone's body grows in unique ways, going through a similar yet different set of significant changes during its lifetime.

When i was about 14 me and some of my friends made a club in honor of our club teens and in hope their bodies would develop into more curvaceous, womanly bodies. This of course happened to every member of the club except for one—me. But i shall not be worried —it could be worse. After all i am healthy and happy and that's what counts because as i was once told by my nanna: Looks fade.
—unstudiedone

here's what I think...your breasts are the size they are, your stomachs are however hairy they are, and any man who gives a rat's ass is not worth your trouble. stop worrying about how your body looks and start doing something worthwhile, how about that? you are all beautiful...the human body is beautiful...
—love_buggie

I love my body just the way it is! I was made in the likeness of Jesus Christ, my Lord and Savior. He created me, and if I say "I hate my boobs, or my nose, or something" I am saying that I hate God's plans or ideas. So it just goes to say —> love your body, cuz it's specially made by God!
—preppygirl04

The bottom line is that no matter how big your boobs are or what you look like there will always be someone who has a body you want more than your own, and chances are that the very same person whose body you admire is wishing they looked more like someone else.
—dustee

I don't really like my arms. I want Britney Spears' arms, in fact, I wouldn't mind having Britney's butt, legs, the list goes ON and ON and ON...
—rocker_chika

i like the old-timey pinup girls from the 50s and i think they look sexy. their bodies are like mine, so that always reassures me.
—juniemoonie

I JUST CAN'T HELP IT. I HATE MYSELF, ESPECIALLY THE BEING FAT PART.
—coccoloco

I have never really been about my weight and I self-conscious have a friend acts who is bigger than me and I am th take a leaf out of but her weight.
—ash182

every-one tells me that i am so skinny but when i look at myself in the mirror i see fat - tons of fat.
—froggyeffie

There are so many different kinds of bodies in the world, and almost all of them have been idealized in different places at different times. Every day we are bombarded by media images of celebrities—mostly actors, models, and pop stars—whose appearances have been carefully constructed for our consumption. We often develop our body images in relation to these media-generated ideals, and they can powerfully influence our feelings about what our bodies should look like. When your natural assets vary from the reigning ideal, it can be harder to maintain a positive image of yourself. If the ideal you're being force-fed at the moment doesn't suit you, try to look for one that does.

WEIGHT AND BODY IMAGE

Weight tends to play a huge role in the body image of many girls, no doubt in response to the exaggerated (and often unhealthy) thin ideal images we are surrounded by. Girls who worry about being too heavy or fat or large often spend an excessive amount of time and energy obsessing and generally feeling bad about themselves, even when other people tell them differently. This is depressing—especially when you think about all the things a person could be doing instead!

No matter how big or small you really are, eating right and exercising are the best things you can do for both your weight and your body image.

In extreme cases (often compounded by psychological issues), weight obsession can intensify and develop into dangerous eating disorders like bulimia and anorexia, in which the sufferer has a seriously distorted self-image, seeing herself as fat no matter how emaciated she is.

FOR MORE ON TAKING CARE OF YOUR BODY, SEE PAGES 40–43

SEE EATING DISORDERS ON PAGES 44–45

Our body image is almost always wrapped up in how we think others—boys, friends, boyfriends, parents, teachers—see us. Compliments or criticisms, even when they are just offhand remarks, can have a huge impact on a person's body image.

People have a tendency to focus and comment on particular body parts, especially when they first develop. If this sounds familiar to you, it's important to keep in mind that you and your body are so much more complex than any one part. Try not to let a certain body part overwhelm your entire body image.

SEE BODY PARTS, PAGES 46–83

When you're a teenager, the pressure to have a boyfriend can be particularly intense and the issue of what boys find attractive often takes on added importance. Of course, it is impossible to generalize about what boys like, as each one has his own preferences.

When others see faults, it can amplify bad feelings you already have or create a whole new sore point. Negative feedback is hard to take and is often really unnecessary. Most of the time people say mean and insulting things as a way of elevating themselves at the expense of others. (This is one of the uglier human traits…)

On the other hand, the way others see you can open you up to a new and positive view of your body or reinforce good feelings you already have. Focusing on aspects of your body that you like can make you feel better about your body as a whole.

BODY DIFFERENCES

While many people have problems with the way their bodies look, some people have to contend with a different set of issues caused by birth defects, disease, or accidents that alter their physical appearance or make it somehow different from the accepted "norm." When your body is not fully intact or functional, it can make the already difficult task of maintaining a positive self-image more challenging. This can be compounded by the fact that people who are disabled or otherwise different are rarely represented in the media, and almost never without focusing on what sets them apart. In reality, whatever is "wrong" or "right" with your body is just one part of the picture—it doesn't define the whole person you are.

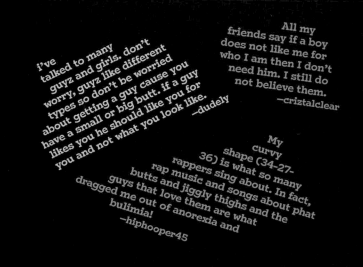

Your body is yours alone. People can influence your feelings about it but ultimately you are in charge. What you do with your body has a huge effect on your body image. Taking good care of it—eating well, exercising, finding ways to relieve stress—is the foundation of feeling good about it.

Our bodies are where we live. Most of what we do with them has nothing to do with how we look, yet a big part of our body image is wrapped up in appearance. The body is an amazing piece of machinery. It does so much for you already, and it can do so much more

APPRECIATING THE BODY

The body is amazing. It has tremendous endurance and resilience; it's self-protective, and can repair itself when injured. It has it own sense memory and can learn new ways of doing things throughout its lifetime. The body's sensory organs (its eyes, ears, nose, mouth, and skin) allow us to experience the beauty and richness that the world has to offer: art, good food, great stories, fun, love... And the body itself creates pleasure, when it is touched in various ways.

than you might imagine. You can learn a lot from your body, especially when you get beyond obsessing about how it looks (which, after all, can get pretty boring). Putting your energy into things you like to do and appreciating your accomplishments instills the kind of self-confidence that can see you through life's inevitable highs and lows—and provide lots of joy in the process!

CHANGING BODIES

Bodies evolve over time. They go through a certain set of changes when they reach maturity and continue to change as we get older. Aging is a natural process—bodies are living things, and all living things have a life cycle. But our culture tends to see aging as a process of loss instead of focusing on the substantial gains of growing older and wiser.

Dealing with the body's aging is difficult for many people. Women can have an especially hard time if they are very focused on our culture's youthful beauty ideal (which is reinforced by thousands of products designed to combat the symptoms of aging as if it were a disease). While youth is a big part of beauty for many in our society, others see things differently, valuing experience and personal strength as part of a woman's appeal.

A lot of girls are self-conscious about their stomachs. Well I've come to the conclusion that guys have big hands for a reason and what may feel big to us (like love handles) doesn't feel big to them. Most guys like girls that have some meat on them b/c they have something to hold on to. So you don't have to have a stomach like Britney Spears to be sexy, just learn to love what you got (I have)! Confidence is more sexy to a guy than a tight stomach.
                                —desidemona

THE BODY IMAGE BLUES

size and shape

Everybody's got a unique size and shape, determined by a number of factors. There is, first of all, your natural bone structure, which can range from long and narrow to short and wide, and anywhere in between. And then there are your body's natural tendencies in terms of muscle tone and fat storage. Body size and shape have a lot to do with your genes, and often run in the family—and can vary by ethnicity.

If (you feel) your body is at an extreme—small, large, short, tall—it may be more challenging to accept its natural state.

What you do with your body, in terms of eating and exercising, also has an effect on your body's shape and size.

SEE TAKING CARE OF YOURSELF, PAGES 40–43, FOR INFO ON HOW TO TREAT YOUR BODY RIGHT!

SIZE AND CULTURE

The thin ideal which persisted for much of 20th-century Western culture has created a certain stigma for large people in our society. However, not everyone subscribes to this viewpoint. Many Latin Americans and African Americans, in particular, value a more curvaceous body, with big butts and hips. A common saying among Latinos is "Bones are for dogs." And in many cultures around the world, largeness is seen as a symbol of sexual maturity, fertility, prosperity, strength, and wisdom. Despite the differing cultural views, weight is a major issue for a lot of girls and women, and often contributes to self-image problems.

OBESITY

Obesity is a condition characterized by excessive body fat—and is now considered one of the biggest health problems facing the U.S. There are a number of suspected causes, including a more sedentary lifestyle and increased marketing and consumption of junk food.

Obesity can have a genetic or hormonal component, which can make it more difficult to lose fat. However, many formerly obese people have lost weight by becoming more active and more conscious about what they are eating.

Actually, I like being short. I take up less space and, if I want, I can get in the front row for group photographs.
—allalexis

SEE PAGE 34 FOR MORE ON WEIGHT AND BODY IMAGE

My nickname is "bird" because I have a fat torso and skinny legs. —black_kitty

my hips are soo wide!! i have a pear shape, skinny with a wide bottom!! —lil_brown_suga

I am a size 12 because I am 6 feet tall and the rest of my body is bigger, including my hips, because of my height. I am not fat, I just have a bigger jeans size because of my big hips. —mandarintheif

I was blessed with my grandmother's short and "stocky" build. I have wide hips and broad shoulders, not to mention large arms. —glitterflitz

Okay, I'm a nice-sized girl—everything about my body, abs, thighs, legs, I seem to be fine about. But when it comes to my hips, there's a whole other issue. I'm latina so the curves are sort of a given. —wandarama

i am thinner than all the other girls and have always been teased for it. worst of all, people think i am anorexic because i am just that skinny! —babeleh

I am a lot taller than all my friends and because I come from a big-boned family. I also have large hipbones. Compared to my friends who are all shorter and skinnier than me, I look huge. —cheerchi03

measurements

Numbers tend to be involved when people talk about dimensions or clothing sizes—and they are easy to use when comparing yourself to other people. Of course, a number could never accurately describe the uniqueness of a person's body. Besides, clothing sizes are often inconsistent: three people can wear the same pants size and have totally different bodies. Sizes vary by brand and don't account for people's different body shapes.

FRUIT SALAD

Lots of folks find that when they do gain weight it all flocks to one area—top or bottom. The "women as fruit" classification system grew out of these tendencies.

APPLES generally store fat in the abdomen and above.

PEARS tend to store fat below the waist, around the hips and on the thighs.

body types

People have developed lots of ways of categorizing the natural differences of our bodies. The thing to remember is that most bodies don't fit neatly into any one category.

THE "MORPHS"

In the 1940s William H. Sheldon divided people into three main body types:

ECTOMORPHS have a long, slender, "beanpole" shape, with narrow hips and shoulders and flat chests. They have a hard time gaining both fat and muscle.

MESOMORPHS are naturally muscular and store fat evenly all over their bodies. They may have broad shoulders and a generally rectangular shape. They can gain or lose both muscle and fat with relative ease.

ENDOMORPHS are soft, round, and curvy. They can build up muscle fairly easily (though not as fast as the mesomorphs), but they have a hard time losing fat.

DOSHAS

A different way of thinking about body types comes from ayurveda, an ancient Indian system of caring for the body and mind. This approach emphasizes three main life energies, called doshas. Everybody has all three doshas, but one or another may be dominant in your particular makeup. Looking and feeling good depend on finding the right dosha balance.

VATA people are full of movement, with lots of creative energy and enthusiasm. They tend to be slender, with small shoulders and hips. Many vatas have a fast metabolism, and it may be hard for them to gain weight. Other vata qualities are angularity and dry hair and skin. Eating warm comfort foods and getting lots of sleep help vatas to stay in balance.

PITTA people exude focus and intelligence. They tend to be of medium build, with good muscle tone. They're sensitive to heat and may sweat a lot. Pittas should not skip meals (and will experience sharp hunger pains if they do). They can benefit from rest and meditation. Eating cool, nonspicy foods (salads and fruit) helps keep pittas' energy balanced. A vegetarian diet is also a good idea.

KAPHA people are strong and sturdy, both physically and psychologically. Their skin tends to be oily, and their body frame is often large. Kapha's metabolism chugs along at a slow and steady pace. They're quicker to put on weight and slower to lose it than vata or pitta folks. Small, lightly cooked, spicy meals can help to rev up their metabolism.

39

taking care of your body

Generally speaking, a healthy diet, regular exercise, and rest will do wonders for your health and your body image. Taking care of yourself will also make you look your best.

dieting

Dieting—especially crash diets—can rob the body of vital vitamins and minerals. On top of that, it doesn't even work!

Human biology works against dieting. We gain fat cells when we're babies and right before puberty, but then the number's pretty much set. Fat cells expand and contract, like balloons. If you diet, the stored fat is used when you need energy, and the fat cells send a message that the body is being deprived of food, so you feel hungry. Also, when you cut back on how much you eat, the body protects itself by slowing its metabolism, so less fat is burned. According to a study by the National Institutes of Health (NIH), 98 percent of dieters who lose weight gain it back within five years, and 90 percent of these gain back more than they lost.

Diets that encourage you to eat lots of a certain food (such as red meat, grapefruit, or cabbage) or eliminate other foods (such as carbohydrates) are dangerous because they throw off the delicate balance in your body, giving you an excess of certain nutrients and depriving you of others. It's also important to recognize that dieting is an industry, and that millions of dollars are spent each year to get you to buy the latest book, pill, powder, protein bar, or piece of exercise equipment.

The only thing that will truly help you to stay fit is treating your body right by eating well and exercising.

WHAT IS A HEALTHY DIET?

The simplest definition of a healthy diet is eating a broad variety of fresh foods. Fresh fruits and vegetables (as well as whole grains) are high in fiber, which cleans out the system. Fish, poultry, and beans are all good choices for protein, which the body needs to grow and rebuild itself. In terms of vitamins, the best strategy is to eat a varied diet. You can talk to your doctor about taking a multivitamin, but the body absorbs vitamins better when they come from foods rather than supplements. Avoid processed foods like white bread and fast foods, which have little to no nutritive value. Also avoid "junk" foods, which tend to be high in saturated (bad) fats and low on nutrition. The body needs a certain amount of fat, and unsaturated (good) fats are much healthier for you.

Since anemia can be a problem for menstruating women and girls, getting enough iron is key. Good iron sources include broccoli, potatoes, kidney beans, red meat, eggs, and whole or enriched ("iron-fortified") grains. It's also important to get enough calcium—from milk, cheese, or yogurt. Another overlooked essential is water. Water accounts for about 60 percent of your body, where it carries nutrients, eliminates waste, and lubricates joints. So drink plenty of it, especially if you're exercising and losing water through perspiration.

In addition to what you eat, it's good to be conscious about when you eat. Letting yourself get too hungry can cause you to lose focus and feel tired or irritated. For most people, three meals with a few snacks in between is the preferred approach. However, some nutritionists recommend (and some people prefer) lots of smaller meals. Whatever works for you is fine as long as you eat when you're hungry and you eat well.

I'm too lazy to exercise and too tempted to stop eating the foods I love. lose weight fast and I need to -i.luv.u.yeah

hey i am fat and every time i try to go on a diet it just backfires and doesn't work! —alienatedme

Almost all of my life, I've been chubby. Since about 7th grade all the way till now, 10th grade, I've been a steady size 18. I used to hate EVERYTHING about my body: the huge spare tire around my middle, my flabby arms, the thighs, everything. I was extremely self-conscious about it since I was teased constantly in grade school. Every diet I tried, I didn't stick to. It got so bad that I didn't even like to go shopping anymore. One day, something inside me snapped. It was like a voice somewhere in my head screamed: "I DON'T WANNA BE LIKE THIS ANYMORE!!" So, I decided to change it. I take walks now with my dog, I've changed my eating habits (my weaknesses were coke & potato chips) & I drink at least 6 bottles of water a day. Now I'm a size 16. That isn't to say I wouldn't love to be a 14 or 12—I would. And I'm working on it. But my point is, once I realized that I controlled my weight, I was able to say no to things that are bad for me. With the help of my mom, who told me straightfor- wardly that I was beautiful, & focusing on things I really like about myself (like my gorgeous hazel eyes, my slender calves, & the fact that I tan naturally) I'm able to love myself. And hey, anybody that says plus- size girls aren't cute, just look at Marilyn Monroe. She was a size 12 & America's sexpot!
—bubblezap

In 6th grade I realized I was a heavy girl. I was never large and in charge, but I was chunky. So I decided to do something about it. There is a YMCA close to my home. So almost every day now for 2 years, I've gone to the Y to work out for about 1 or 2 hours. It has really begun to show. My self-confi- dence is up, and I lost 2 dress sizes. This just goes to show that all those diets can't beat eating right and exercising.
—lil_trackstar

exercise

Exercise is the human body's natural state, as we are designed to move and to be highly active. Regular exercise has amazing benefits. It normalizes the appetite, helping you maintain (or lose) weight by burning calories. It improves your circulatory and respiratory systems. It also strength- ens muscles and increases bone density. People who exercise tend to live longer and get sick less frequently because exercise boosts the immune system. Exercise is also a great way to relieve stress.

In addition to all of the physical benefits, exercise can make you feel good— in part because your body releases "feel-good chemicals" called endorphins and in part because you just look better. Also, there is something innately great about being able to appreciate your body for its ability to be strong, flexible, quick, balanced, coordinated, et cetera.

Unfortunately, in these modern, automated times, lots of people get less exer- cise than at any other point in our history. It is far too easy to spend most of our time watching TV, sitting in front of the computer, driving, and doing other things that don't involve movement.

If you don't exercise regularly, it may seem intimidating to get into an exercise routine. There is not one kind of exercise that is best or right. Whatever makes you feel good, for whatever reason, is a good place to start. Find anything you enjoy doing that requires your body to move. For some people, it's sports like soccer, basketball, skating, tennis, or swimming. For others, it's activities like yoga, hiking, martial arts, pilates, dancing, or even gardening. The American College of Sports Medicine recommends exercising 30 to 45 minutes three to five times a week. But the point of exercise is less about a rigid schedule and more about leading a generally active life.

There are three basic types of exercise: stretch- ing, aerobic (or cardiovascular) exercise, and strength training. All three elements are important for overall fitness: Stretching improves flexibility and range of motion. Aerobic exercise—anything that increases the heart rate—is good for your heart, lungs, and whole respiratory system. And strength training builds muscles.

JUNK FOOD

Junk foods are foods with very little protein, vitamins, or minerals. Most of the calories in these foods come from sugars and fats, which, along with salt, are among the top three ingredients in the worst junk foods. Soda, in particular, has been linked to tooth decay, obesity, caffeine dependence, and bone weakening. Most carbonated beverages are high in phosphates, which leach calcium from the bones. Another con- cern is that if kids eat too much junk food when they are young, they risk an early onset of type 2 diabetes and heart disease.

Recently, legislators in Texas and California have taken steps to eliminate junk foods from their school cafeterias. In some states, a sin tax (like the tax on ciga- rettes) is being considered for junk foods.

downward
dog

BODY CONSCIOUSNESS

The mind affects the body and the body affects the mind—this is known as the mind/body connection. The idea is that how you feel in your body has a lot to do with how you feel about yourself in general.

Certain types of exercise or movement are particularly good for helping you to connect with your body. You can look for classes, books, or videos on any of the following. It's always a good idea to start with some sort of instruction before going off on your own, to be sure you don't hurt yourself.

YOGA: Yoga is a mind-body practice that developed in India over 5,000 years ago and has been evolving ever since. Physically, yoga involves doing poses called asanas that stretch and strengthen muscles, improving flexibility, strength, and endurance. (See some poses on this page.) It can also help to reduce stress and tension and improve concentration. There are lots of different styles of yoga, ranging from the spiritual (which includes breathing exercises and meditation) to the athletic, as well as combinations of the two.

TAI CHI: Tai chi is a "martial art" developed in China by Taoist monks who needed to defend themselves while maintaining their health and spiritual growth. It is a choreographed series of movements called a "form," and the aim is to remain in a middle state between two opposing forces and to use only enough energy for each move. The exercises are deceptively simple and involve breathing naturally, moving slowly, visualizing energy moving through the body, and focusing on what the Chinese call the **tantien**, the energy center located below and behind the navel. Tai Chi helps people to harness their inner energy, improving balance, immunity, and reflexes.

tree

PILATES: A form of exercise used by dancers to build strength without bulk, Pilates can help improve coordination, posture, strength, flexibility, and body awareness. Pilates focuses on developing concentration, control, and breathing techniques, and building core muscle strength. Pilates exercises can be done on special resistance machines or on floor mats.

cobra

resting and relaxing

As important as it is to be active, it's also crucial to relax. Teenagers in particular need to get lots of sleep. A lack of sleep can have an impact on your concentration, judgment, and mood.

In addition to sleep, it is important to find ways to relieve the stress in your life. Exercise is a great way to do this, as are the following activities.

MEDITATION

Meditation is an ancient technique used to help clear your thoughts, become more focused, and relax. The process usually involves a series of different practices to slow down your breathing: First, sit down on the floor, keeping your back as straight as possible. Close your eyes and listen to yourself breathe. Sometimes it is helpful to count your breaths or repeat a single word, phrase, or sound (whether it's "om" or something else). The goal is to empty your mind of any clutter and concentrate simply on breathing.

Visualization can also be helpful. Picture yourself in a quiet, tranquil setting, like by a stream or on the beach. Focus only on what you see in this place, disregarding any thoughts that may distract you from the serenity. Proper meditation takes a lot of practice, and results are never immediate. Over time it can lead to lower blood pressure, lower stress, and a clearer mind.

AROMATHERAPY

Different smells can have different effects on our minds and our moods. Pleasant scents can cause the secretion of certain kinds of hormones like serotonin, which tells our bodies to relax. Aromatherapy uses essential oils—scents taken from flowers, leaves, seeds, or fruit that are compressed and distilled into oils. Relaxing essential oils include chamomile, cypress, frankincense, jasmine, lavender, marjoram, rose, and sandalwood. These oils can be put in aroma lamps, humidifiers, baths, or body lotion to relax the mind and soothe the body.

FOR RESOURCES ON TAKING CARE OF YOUR BODY, SEE PAGE 149

MASSAGE

Throughout history, almost every culture has used the power of touch to heal. Massage reduces stress and stimulates the body to heal itself. It's best to get a massage from a licensed massage therapist (LMT), but even rubbing (or having somebody else rub) your own feet will feel good. There are many types of massages—including Swedish, shiatsu, deep tissue, and lymphatic—which use different techniques to heal and relax the body.

not taking care of your body

Not taking care of yourself can range from passive, easily reversible habits such as eating poorly to self-destructive behaviors such as cutting. Becoming more conscious about your behavior can help you to make healthier choices. If you're hurting yourself, you first need to understand why before you can change. Talking to a professional—a school counselor, a therapist, or a physician—is often an essential part of this process.

eating disorders

For women and girls, eating disorders are the most common form of self-destruction. In the U.S., where a bone-thin body type is idealized by the media, the average model is 5 feet 9 inches tall and weighs 123 pounds while the average American woman is 5 feet 4 1/2 inches tall and weighs 142 pounds. Some of the 2 million Americans who suffer from eating disorders are probably affected by these media messages. Other causes may include the desire to feel in control or to punish parents. An eating disorder can also be a cry for help.

Taking diet pills, laxatives, or diuretics—as well as following extreme fad diets—are all risky behaviors, even if there's not a distinct name for these activities. In extreme cases, people can starve themselves to death or overeat to the extent that they bring on life-threatening illnesses. There are many types of eating disorders, all requiring professional medical care.

ANOREXIA NERVOSA

Anorexics have a distorted perception of their bodies that leads them to severely restrict food intake, to the point of deliberate starvation. Even when they're emaciated, anorexics believe they are fat. Often perfectionists, they need to control their weight—this is a big part of their condition. The severe weight loss that accompanies anorexia can lead to all sorts of physical problems including irregular periods, thinning hair on the head, growth of downy hair on the body, low body temperature and blood pressure, slowed reflexes, swollen joints, and in severe cases kidney and heart failure, which can be fatal.

BULIMIA

Bulimia is binge eating followed by purging (through vomiting or taking laxatives or diuretics). The binge—which can range from a single cookie to enormous amounts of food—is usually done in secret, as is the purging. Bulimics are rarely overweight, although they often have a distorted sense of their body size. For many, there can be shame associated with their lack of control when eating, and purging may help to restore their sense of control. Bulimia may lead to irregular periods, constipation, damaged and discolored teeth, heartburn, lung and kidney damage, salivary gland enlargement, and other conditions caused by the repeated vomiting.

BINGE EATING DISORDER

Binge eaters, most of whom are obese, go on periodic binges (maybe twice a week), uncontrollably consuming huge quantities of food in short periods of time. Unlike bulimics, bingers don't purge afterward. Although the causes are unknown, up to half of all people with binge eating disorder have a history of depression. Bingers may eat for emotional reasons—to comfort themselves, to avoid threatening situations—or simply because they're hungry from dieting. Binge eaters may have severe weight gains or fluctuations, swollen limbs, high blood pressure and/or blood cholesterol, as well as all of the diseases that accompany obesity such as diabetes and heart disease.

self-mutilation

There are a range of behaviors in which people deliberately, repetitively, impulsively harm themselves. Some common forms of self-mutilation include:

FACE PICKING

HAIR PULLING (also known as trichotillomania)

CUTTING

CARVING words or pictures into the body using razors, knives, paper clips, pens, fingernails, or anything else sharp

Sometimes self-mutilation is the result of alcohol or drug abuse, physical or sexual abuse, or an eating disorder. To people who are depressed, anxious, or angry, self-inflicted pain may distract them from some other unbearable feeling. Many people who self-mutilate suffer from "dissociation"—a feeling of being outside of the body. Other cutters, unable to express anger or pain in a healthy way, turn their bad feelings on themselves. Whatever the reason, it's important to get professional help, and it's essential to stop.

FOR RESOURCES ON EATING DISORDERS AND SELF-MUTILATION, SEE PAGE 150

COMPULSIVE OVEREATING

In contrast to binge eating, compulsive overeating involves constant eating—also without the purging typical of bulimia. Compulsive overeaters have an "addiction" to food, and they eat for emotional rather than nutritional reasons, often consuming huge quantities of junk food for comfort. These patterns of behavior start in early childhood, so most compulsive eaters have never learned how to properly cope with stress. Symptoms overlap with those of binge eating disorder and include constipation, muscle atrophy, and a puffy look from poor circulation.

UNHEALTHY SUPPORT

In the last few years a number of websites have appeared that act as support groups for girls with eating disorders. While this may sound like a good idea, these girls are often actually supporting each other in life-threatening behaviors.

drugs and addiction

While a person may not start taking drugs with self-destructive motivations, drug use can put your body in harm's way. For this reason, it is important to understand the dangers associated with specific drugs and the greater risk of addiction. Most drugs are harmful to your body when taken in extremes.

Some drugs, like heroin and Special K, can be fatal on the first try. Others, such as cocaine and methamphetamine, are highly addictive. Drug addiction is debilitating and physically dangerous, and it can ruin families and lives.

SMOKING

Cigarette smoking is the single worst thing you can do for your health and is the number one cause of preventable deaths in the U.S. People who start smoking as teens put themselves at higher risk for addiction. In addition to increasing your risk for cancer and heart disease (and birth defects, if you smoke while pregnant), smoking discolors teeth and nails, and increases wrinkles around your mouth. It can also lead to early menopause.

body parts

Your overall body and beauty image is affected by how you feel about its various parts. Often people focus on specific body parts as points of beauty, as in somebody's "beautiful eyes," "great legs," or "nice butt." But beauty is so much more than the sum of the parts.

There are lots of factors at work when it comes to your relationships with your body parts. First, there's heredity. Our parents' genes often manifest themselves in a certain body part. Some traits run in the family and some run within different ethnic groups.

One of the nice things about body parts is that there are so many of them. If, for whatever reason, you feel bad about a particular body part, it's usually not that hard to find another one to feel good about.

Some body parts, like boobs and butts, are more associated with sexuality, and so can seem particularly loaded—especially if you feel like yours are too little or too big.

I have the same ugly feet as my mom—wide with short, stubby toes.
-artluvr17

I'm actually really happy with my hair. I know this sounds weird, sometimes I think it's like a prerequisite for girls to hate their hair (and sometimes I just say I do hate my hair so as not to stick out)!
-animeartz

I look nothing like my mother, and I don't resemble my siblings, but my eyes, a gift from my father, tell me that yes, I am a true member of the family.
-incubus_99

One of my best guy friends, Kevin, is more confident about his hairstyle than anyone I know. He probably has the most unkempt head of hair I have ever seen, but he is always running his fingers through it and saying, "I love my hair!" It is hard to tease him about it when it doesn't faze him at all! When I'm with Kevin, his self-esteem makes me feel gorgeous too!
-bottlegenie

my butt is huge. i have tried everything to hide it or make it look smaller. then one day in 9th grade, this guy i had been crushing on since 7th grade complimented me on my butt. he said it was perfect and i should keep it that way. now i'm in 11th grade and i love my butt!!

—millenium

I think my boobs are too small but it doesn't bother me much because I have a couple of friends who are the same way and we laugh about it.

—zoiinkerz

over my rear. Now I've gained a bit of perspective. My generous posterior is a slap in the face of those who think you've got to be stick-thin to be pretty. While I am very short, my hourglass figure ensures that nobody will ever mistake me for a child. Plus, my girlfriend says that one of her favorite things about me is the curve of my hips. Point is, rather than finding things wrong with your body, choose to see them as distinctive. If you think you're lovely, you will be,

—LaDaRu

I have what a friend once described as "child-bearing hips." Were these ancient times, I would fetch a high price from matchmakers. These days of Thunder look somewhat incongruous on me, a petite and slender girl who just barely scrapes the five-foot mark. I used to hate them. I'd spend hours in dressing rooms, rejecting jeans that fit my legs beautifully but could not be forced

If it seems that any of your body parts do not fit in with the ideal of the moment, it can be discouraging. It may help to remember that at various times and in various places, almost every shape, size, and kind of body part has been considered beautiful. Besides, the fact that we all look different keeps things interesting, and the specific shape and proportion of your body is part of what makes you unique.

Our bodies go through lots of changes on the journey from childhood to adulthood. And so does our consciousness. Something that may feel abnormal or out of place at one point may begin to feel beautiful over time. If you're not fully grown, your body parts may not be either. Or they may seem out of proportion to the rest of you. Certain body parts (like noses and legs) can grow particularly fast and it can take a while for the rest of your body to catch up.

Accepting the body parts that aren't your favorites may not happen overnight. If you have to fend off teasing and negativity, it can make it even harder. But in most cases, self-acceptance is just waiting for you to find it.

Knowing that other people share your issues can help you to be more accepting. Sometimes the thing that makes you change your mind about a body part is realizing that other people appreciate it, even if you don't. Living with a body part for a long time can and often does change your relationship to it. Body parts literally grow on you...sometimes to the extent that something you once hated becomes a point of pride.

My arms...ICK. For many years of my life I would wear long sleeves...even in the summer when it was hot, because I didn't want anyone to see my upper arms because I thought that they were disgusting. One day I spilled juice all over myself at school. I only had a strappy tank top to change into. I was really self-conscious about the outfit, but my friend convinced me that if I didn't make a big deal about it, no one would. And you know what, she was right. No one cares about my arm flab. So I kissed the long sleeves good-bye and wear whatever tops I choose to wear.

—kiwistar

At first I never noticed my nose. And then someone made a comment. At first I felt so bad that I didn't have the normal, small, cutesy turned-up little nose, but then I looked at myself in the mirror one day and realized what I am. I am not the cute, blonde, skinny, blue-eyed, and small-nosed cheerleader type. I am exotic-looking, and no one can compare with me. Sometimes you just have to look at the feature you hate the most about yourself and think about how it makes you feel individual and different. It makes YOU YOU!!!

—roxybluesky

hair

Hair is one of the most immediately noticeable elements of a person's body. It carries lots of different meanings all at once, depending on someone's religion, ethnicity, social circle, or frame of mind—and it can be seen as a sexual symbol (especially when it's long and untamed). All of these things and more contribute to making hair a major looks fixation for lots of people.

The color, texture, and thickness of your hair are determined by your genes and can vary by ethnicity. For example, Mediterranean hair is often dark and curly, Scandinavian blond and straight, Asian black and fine, and African dark and kinky.

HAIR COLOR

Some people's hair color naturally changes over time, usually getting darker as they grow from blond babies to brown-headed teens. Staying out in the sun for a significant period of time can lighten your hair. And, of course, there is a whole range of products used to color hair, from henna to highlights to bleaching to permanent color.

I bleach it blond cuz I like the look.
-blondie88

SEE DECORATING THE BODY, PAGE 84, FOR MORE ON HAIR DYE

I think people who dye their hair are fake.
-guitargirlie

Over the summer my hair was blue. For school i had to bleach it out, which took lots of bleach because the stuff was stubborn. SO now i have to use LOTS of DEEP conditioning every day.
-infinity8

I usually keep my hair in braids, which are a total gift from God. There is absolutely no hassle about it.
-bowtothequeen

HAIR THICKNESS AND TEXTURE

As with color, the texture of your hair—whether it's straight, wavy, curly, or kinky—is genetic, and so is the thickness. Hair texture and thickness can sometimes change as you age or after pregnancy or illness. Some women decide to leave their hair as is. Others use hair products such as gel, mousse, or volumizer to give the appearance of thicker or smoother hair. People also use different processes and tools (relaxers or perms; blow-dryers, rollers, or irons) to temporarily transform the texture of their hair, going from straight to wavy or curly—or vice versa. You've got to experiment to find the products, tools, and techniques that work for you.

Although models and actors who are filmed or photographed in studios don't have to worry about the weather, the climate does affect the way your hair looks. Humidity, in particular, can make hair frizzy. There is a huge range of products that are specifically designed to control frizz.

i just dyed it red. Now i'm fiery!
-chixstix

My hair is usually frizzy and thick. What's weird is that if i just put some gel or hairspray in it and scrunch it, letting it dry naturally, it gets really curly without frizz.
-sassafrasslass

My hair is really straight and thin. People used to make fun of me because it would get stringy if I didn't brush it. I learned to love my hair. I just use mousse and volumizing shampoo to pump it up. Some days I leave it straight for a laid-back look.
-canadiansweetie

The Afro

In the first half of the 20th century, many African American women, and some men, straightened their hair with heat treatments or chemicals such as lye (and many still do). The afro or "a natural" became the hairstyle of choice for many African Americans during the black pride movement of the 1960s. Fueled by the civil rights movement and a sense of ethnic pride and identity, many blacks allowed their hair to grow in its natural state. Civil rights activists, like Angela Davis and Stokely Carmichael, as well as entertainers like Jimi Hendrix and Roberta Flack, all sported afros during this time. The afro became a popular look for non-blacks with super-curly hair as well, with stars like Barbra Streisand sporting the 'fro. Though the afro had its heyday from the mid-60s to the mid-70s, it has achieved classic hairstyle status and remains popular today.

HAIR LENGTH

People's hair grows at different rates and can have different maximum lengths. Usually it doesn't grow more than three feet long. Hair grows fastest during your teens and early twenties.

Hair can be lengthened with a weave, extensions or braids. The process, which involves sewing, gluing or braiding synthetic or human hair into your own hair, takes hours (up to a whole day) and can be expensive. The results can last for several months. A hairpiece that can be attached by clip or comb, or around a ponytail, is a quick, less costly alternative.

In recent history, it was the fashion for women to keep their hair long and for men to wear theirs short. There were plenty of exceptions to this, mostly having to do with men's ceremonial wear. Eighteenth-century English and Revolutionary-era American politicians both wore long wigs. The 1920s flapper era marked one of the first times in Western fashion when short hair on women was upheld as a style ideal—and as a symbol of political and social freedom for women. The flapper's quintessential short bob created an unprecedented demand for beauty parlors, which increased in number from 5,000 in 1920 to 25,000 in 1925. In general, during the 20th century, the relationship between hair length and gender unwound. In the 1960s the widespread adoption of hippie style made it much more acceptable for men to wear long hair. And today the question of short versus long hair on guys or girls is mostly a matter of personal preference.

My hair is short, it does not grow fast enough, i have had it short for sooooo long, and i wish it would grow faster!!! i hate it!
—swimmyswim

My hair is now about 26 inches long, and I'm letting it get longer. Another year and it'll be past my butt! I think it's sexy having your hair long.
—thelilleah

My hair was terrible when I wore it long, because it made my face look so long! So I chopped it all off. I now wear it short and spiky, and it suits me so much better.
—HickoryNut

My hair used to be a frizzy, huge mess until i started using volumizing mousse and learned how to use a diffuser. Now it looks gorgeous and everyone asks if the ringlets are natural and how i do it!
—zoolandia

My hair is ultra-fine, so fine it gets really limp. I try to give it more body, but to no avail. So I just keep it short and have it layered and angled.
—zebrastripy

my hair is the most versatile and entertaining part of me, with the most possibilities to show how odd i dare to be. i shaved it bald last year...even the lack of it was fun! my stubble that grew in felt as fuzzy as a bunny. :) i have dyed it purple, pink, and green. once i learned to think of hair as "just hair" i have had endless fun with it.
—anarchobabe

My hair is more like a big, brown, hairy mess than anything else. I like it because it makes me unique from the array of flatness.
—laker_lover

HAIR AND IDENTITY

Why is it that some people seem comfortable with their natural hair, while others would rather transform it into something totally different? Desire to be different, response to fashion or cultural pressure, and good old laziness are all factors in making the decision of whether or not to let it be. While some people change their hair in the interest of experimentation or fashion, others seem to want to transform their identity. Some girls and women refuse to be seen in public without their naturally curly hair straightened, feeling that they look "ugly" without putting hours of work into taming their hair. Others spray and tease their hair to add body to what they think is unflattering flatness. Any way you feel comfortable styling your hair is ultimately fine, but it might be worth considering the natural look occasionally to give your hair a rest, and to give yourself time to think about what it means to be you without someone else's hairdo.

49

HAIRSTYLING AROUND THE WORLD

The elegantly braided hairstyles in pictures of ancient Egyptian women are wigs made of human hair, horsehair, or lamb's wool. Both women and men shaved their heads to keep them clean and cool. Hair shaving was also common practice among numerous tribes in Africa. Some African women would shave their heads and then let the hair grow back according to a specific pattern outlined in chalk on their scalps.

In Central Africa, Mangbetu women were distinguished by thin braids circling a crownlike metal frame, held in place by long pins of bone. Young Hopi Indian women arranged their hair in squash-blossom loops, creating butterfly-like wings on either side of the head. And geishas in Japan fashioned ornate hair sculptures.

At various points in time, women were forbidden from showing their hair. In the first century, a married Roman woman faced divorce if she uncovered her hair in public. During the Middle Ages, European women were forbidden to show their hair in public so they wore hats and bonnets.

During the Renaissance, styles became much more free-flowing and women were once again permitted to show off their hair in public. In the 1600s French hairstyles became extremely ornate, with adornments ranging from flowers to birdcages. In late-18th-century Europe, wealthy women wore such extravagantly high hairdos that they had to crouch to fit inside carriages. These arrangements, which were built over horsehair pads or wire cages, were typically decorated with feathers, ribbons, or jewels. The doorway to St. Paul's Cathedral in London was actually raised several feet so that women with hair extending up to three feet over their heads could enter. At this point in time, hairdressing became a profession—held mostly by men who had been trained as wig makers.

Hair came down to a more practical level in the 19th century throughout the Western world, although high hair did came back in style in the 1950s. The 1956 invention of the aerosol spray can paved the way for gravity-defying beehives and bouffants held up and in place by hairspray. (Aerosol sprays may have been good for high hairdos, but they were bad for the environment.) Hairspray, gels, and mousses continue to bring hair to new heights today.

HAIRSTYLES

Hair carries a lot of weight and can convey many different meanings. Playing with your hairstyle is one of the quickest ways to change your overall look. You can experiment with color, length, and texture in any combination, being as subtle or dramatic as you like. Wigs allow you to try on every imaginable color and style regardless of your natural hair situation. You can use hair accessories (from pigtail holders and scrunchies to bobby pins and barrettes) to shape your hair in different ways from braids to buns.

Some girls get really into this kind of experimentation, while others get frustrated because they don't get the results they want, and still others prefer not to deal with their hair at all. Some women make bold statements by cutting off their hair or even shaving their heads. Some people like to change their hairstyles with trends or moods, and others find a look they like and stay with it forever. And some others prefer to just let their hair make the decision for them—the "nonstyle" is one of the most popular styles of all. To each her own...

i think my hair is very pretty but it is so thick that if i try to do something with it it takes about an hour or two and that is way too long to be spending on hair.
-blondie88

I change my hair constantly—different colors, different lengths. Right now I like it short and very stylish!
-mymamamia

One of the most talked-about heads of hair was that of movie star Veronica Lake in the early 1940s. Many women tried to imitate the way her locks fell seductively across one eye, but this became a health hazard when women—who'd taken over men's factory jobs to help out during World War II—kept getting their hair caught in machines. The government asked Veronica Lake to change her hairstyle to set an example for other women.

HAIR ISSUES

A major source of hair problems is hair abuse, whether it's overstyling with hair-frying blow-dryers and irons, harsh chemical treatments (bleaching, coloring, perming, relaxing, whatever), or overzealous brushing, teasing, tugging, or yanking. Your hair, like your skin, reflects the overall health of your body, so eating well is important. Crash diets as well as excess sugar and caffeine can have negative effects on the look and feel of your hair.

Flakiness

White flakes falling out of your hair may be the sign of a dry scalp, dandruff, or a skin disorder called seborrheic dermatitis (essentially a more severe form of dandruff). If the flakes are tiny and dry, the problem is probably a dry scalp, but if they're larger and greasy you may have dandruff, which is thought to be caused by overactivity of a particular kind of yeast, sending the dead-cell turnover rate on top of your head into overdrive. Dandruff shampoos may be helpful. But if the problem is severe, it's best to check it out with a doctor.

Hair Loss

On average, we lose 75 to 100 strands of hair a day. Every so often, we go through normal molting phases, where we shed a bunch of hair to make room for new hair. But if there are thin spots on your scalp or huge clumps of hair come out, check with a doctor. Hair loss may stem from your genes, a hormonal imbalance, a more serious medical condition such as lupus, eating disorders, or extreme stress.

Trichotillomania is a hair-pulling disorder that is a form of self-mutilation. Sufferers have a strong and constant urge to pull out their hair, mostly from the scalp, but sometimes from other parts of the body as well. As many as 10 million people in the United States may be plagued with this urge, but effective therapy and drug treatments are available. .

FOR RESOURCES ON TRICHOTILLOMANIA, SEE PAGE 150

I love my hair! It is raven black.
—blubugbaby

I really like my hair. I don't put gel or hairspray in it. And if I have a bad hair day it goes up in a ponytail.
—flipfloppin

Hair and Religion

Religions often have very specific rules regarding head hair. Orthodox Judaism and conservative Islam subscribe to the idea that hair is a symbol of sexuality and require women to cover their hair outside the home. Some traditional Orthodox Jewish women wear wigs called "sheitels" to conceal their hair in public. Buddhist boys who become novice monks and Buddhist girls who become nuns shave off all their hair. Sikh men, who are forbidden to cut their hair, wear it bundled up and covered in a turban.

Hair Myths

A lot of myth and lore surrounds women's hair. In the fairy tale, Rapunzel can only be rescued from the tower by literally letting down her long hair—unwinding 75 feet of golden tresses (a scientific impossibility). Mermaids and sirens are depicted combing their long hair while luring men to their doom. Hair is also seen as a source of strength. Zitkala-Sa, a Sioux writer, described how, as a young girl in the late 19th century, she lost her "spirit" when white missionaries at a boarding school clipped off her braids. In the Old Testament story of Samson and Delilah, Samson, a warrior who was given extraordinary physical powers by God, loses his strength and gets captured when Delilah cuts off his hair.

My best friend and the other women in her family NEVER EVER cut their hair. It's a religious thing. I've known her for about two years and ever since I met her I haven't cut my hair (except for trims).
—soccerbabe

eyes

Eyes are "the windows to the soul."
—PLINY, ANCIENT ROME

Everybody's eyes are distinctive.
Differences in color, shape, size, and the space between the eyes all contribute to people's unique eye looks. Eyes are our most identifiable features, which is why computer programs for face recognition focus on them rather than the nose or the mouth.

Eyes reveal our reactions and emotions through factors like the direction and speed of eye movements, the opening and closing of the pupils, and the positioning of the eyebrows.

EYESIGHT

Over 100 million people in the U.S. have vision problems—are near-sighted, far-sighted, have astigmatism. Most of these conditions are correctable with contact lenses or glasses. New laser surgery procedures that correct vision by permanently altering the shape of the eye are not recommended until the age of 21, as eyes may still be growing and changing until then.

my eyes are REALLY small, and I LOVE THEM. -sunshinein

theyCHANGEfromBROWNtoGREENto GOLDENtoYELLOWinTHEsunlight. ILIKEmyEYES. -buffbuffy

Well, I am Asian...and proud, yet there are a few drawbacks. I have what they call "slant eyes." When I was in elementary school kids would constantly call me names or do the "Chinese Eye Thing." (I'm not even Chinese!) I was emotionally hurt by their comments. As I got older, I realized I loved my eyes because they distinguished me. -clanissa

If there's one thing that I really like about myself, it's my eyes. They're baby blue with navy rims and some navy flecks in them. -queenfaery

The Evil Eye

The eye has a powerful place in myth and magic. Historically, people around the world have believed that they could be seriously harmed by the evil eye, a look from someone arising out of jealousy or spite. In Turkey, parents still hide newborn infants for 40 days to avoid any possibility of an evil eye landing on their babies. Old-time Europeans put prayers in lockets to defend themselves against the evil eye. Indian women used eye makeup to draw black lines around their eyes to protect themselves.

i do have to say that i like my eyes. :) they aren't the ordinary brown eyes (no offense to ppl w/ brown eyes) and they aren't the ever-wanting blue eyes that a lot of ppl wish they had. My eyes are green, and a pretty green at that. some ppl i know even call me "the girl w/ green eyes" when they can't remember my name, which i think is cool. :) -thedreamlives

My eyes are this really light color of baby blue with a ring of green right next to my pupil. They really stand out. Some kid even told me that i had "freaky eyes," but i took that as a compliment. -soccerstar

EYE LOOKS

From ancient times women have used eye makeup to transform their eyes in any number of ways (making them bigger, smaller, lighter, darker, et cetera), bringing attention to them and creating various illusions, from the cat eye to the smoky eye to the mod eye and much more.

EYEBROWS

Eyebrows help stop sweat from running into the eyes. They also reveal a lot about how we're feeling—rising in surprise, lowering with displeasure, scrunching in concentration, shrugging in indifference.

Glasses Fashion

Glasses can contribute a lot to an overall look. Invented in the late 13th century, they have their own style history. Some glasses have achieved classic status.

Sunglasses are great eye protectors, helping to prevent eye disease, while adding an element of mystery, glamour, or playfulness.

nerd glasses

john lennon glasses

cat-eye frames

EYELASHES

Each eye is surrounded by about 200 eyelashes, which last 3 to 5 months before falling out and being replaced. They help protect the eye from dirt.

PUPIL

The pupil is the black hole that lets more or less light into the eye. The wider the pupil, the more light the eye is letting in. This widening and narrowing makes the pupil the most expressive part of the eye. Pupils reach their maximum size during adolescence and then begin to shrink with age. In the 1800s dilated (wide-open) pupils were thought to be more attractive. Women used drops of the poison belladonna to enlarge their pupils, even though this carried the risk of blindness.

IRIS

The iris, the colored part of the eye, is a set of muscles that works to open and close the pupil. The iris is not a single flat tone but rather a variety of hues arranged in a unique pattern of lines and wedge shapes (rods and cones) around the pupil. That's why some people's eyes seem to change color. No two people have the same iris pattern, so iris identification may soon replace fingerprinting as the authoritative way to identify people.

SCLERA

The sclera, the white part of the eye, highlights the eye's expressiveness and allows us to read the movements (and the message) of the contrasting iris and pupil.

nose

Renaissance artist Leonardo da Vinci claimed that the nose determined the character of the face. Jutting out from the face, the nose is one of the most prominent facial features. And it comes in a variety of shapes and sizes—large or small, curved or straight, wide or narrow, flat or bumped.

The nose filters the air you take in, cleaning, warming, and moistening it. It also allows you to identify some 4,000 different odors (women are generally more sensitive to smell than men). Some scientists suggest that the sense of smell is the most powerful of the senses. Smell also plays a role in attraction: pheromones, scents produced by glands in a woman's armpits and genitals, act as sexual attractors. Perfume, cologne, and scented oil are sometimes used for similar effect.

Scientists have lots of theories about why our noses look the way they do and why there are such marked differences in nose shape in different parts of the world. In part, they believe that noses evolved to deal with different climates. For example, in cold areas, people were at an advantage if they had longer noses, which gave the body more time to warm inhaled air before it reached the lungs.

My nose has this bump right in the middle, which for a while i wanted to get shaved off through plastic surgery. But recently strangers have been telling me i look like Isabella Rossellini. Now i like my nose more!
—beautifulwitch

My nose has always been really "distinctive." I remember in the seventh grade, in art class, my friend drew a picture of me and she made my nose jumping out of my body like the Wicked Witch of the West. But now I've learned to love being the "girl with the nose!"
—partypiper

I actually like my nose. It's the right size for my face.
—hestermilf

NOSES AROUND THE WORLD

Throughout history, people from different cultures have tried to reshape or decorate their noses. Nose studs from 4,500 years ago have been found in what is now Pakistan. Seeing flat noses as beautiful, Polynesians deliberately broke their noses to flatten them, while Australian Natives pierced the septum (the part between the nostrils) and put a bony stick in the hole to widen the nose. The San Blas Indian women of Panama, who find giant noses extremely beautiful, paint black lines down their noses to make them appear longer.

CHANGING YOUR NOSE

Maybe because it's smack in the middle of the face, the nose is a feature that people often want to change. Celebrity noses are often touched up for photo shoots, with makeup applied for the express purpose of making the nose seem shorter and narrower.

The only way to change the nose shape permanently is to have rhinoplasty surgery, otherwise known as a nose job. Rhinoplasty is one of the rare kinds of cosmetic surgery done more often on young women in their teens or early twenties than on older women. The reason is that younger skin is more flexible and so more likely to adjust to a new nose shape. During the procedure, the doctor often breaks the nose and reshapes it. Although the surgery is usually performed in a couple of hours at the doctor's office, it takes at least two weeks for the swelling to go down and six months before the injury totally heals.

Some people are happy with the results of a nose job; some are not. Some people end up with a pinched or a droopy look or find it harder to breathe. Because noses are so central to the look of a face, changing your nose may alter your sense of who you are and make all your other features seem strange.

snout beak bugle

when i think of my nose, i shudder! it's small, and pointy. aw well, i'm getting used to it. not like i'm gonna spend the money to "fix" it...
—Jerseygirl

It's somewhat bigger than most people's. It's just because i have a "bump" at the top. Of course, i get teased about it once in a while, but i'm proud of my nose. It's strong. It makes me different from all those girls with perfectly straight, thin noses. It's my Polish heritage nose.
—horsyhoney

You could say my nose

I'm not really into my nose, but it's a part of me. And I love me. I have to learn to accept it, no matter what. I have my nose pierced, so it's pretty cute now that I have a little diamond stud there!
—animegirl

My nose is blackhead city.
—hunny_bunny

I can't stand my nose! In school, some people will call me a bird. It's really pointy. I know I'm going to get a nose job done when I'm older!
—kittykat2002

my mom told me that when she had a sonogram when she was 18 weeks pregnant, all you could see was my nose. at that moment she decided "forget about college...i'm gonna hafta save up for a nose job." however, i finally grew into my nose and i get to go to college after all.
—rubydeedee

BLACKHEADS TEND TO CONGREGATE ON THE NOSE. SEE ACNE ON PAGE 77 FOR MORE INFO.

before

after

in pictures, my nose looks humongous. i want a nose job but i don't want to end up looking like michael jackson.
—XxotiffanyoxX

I've always been a little sensitive about my nose. It's not so bad now, but when I was younger, my nose was too big for my face. I hated it, and I said I was going to get plastic surgery. As soon as I got out of my plastic-surgery phase, my brother told me I needed a nose job! Leave it to siblings...
—queens.baby

My nose is rather prominent. I don't like it. I have small eyes and small lips....then I have this big honker thing in the middle of my face. It just doesn't go.
—Hawaiianhulao

I kind of want my nose shortened when I get older but sometimes I think it's one of my trademarks.
—pop_rocks17

sniffer honker snoot schnoz

mouth

The mouth eats, tastes, talks, kisses, and expresses your feelings, changing its shapes in so many ways. Human mouths are proportionally smaller than most other animals' mouths, and there is a gender difference: female lips tend to be a bit bigger than male lips. Lips have fewer layers of skin than the rest of the body, so more blood vessels show through, giving them their red color. During sexual arousal, the lips moisten, swell, and appear even redder, as blood flow increases.

When I was younger kids used to make fun of me cause they said I had big lips. Now that I've grown into them I haven't met one person who hasn't said how great they are.
–snowprincess

My mouth is truly the smallest one you will ever see. It measures less than an inch in width. The smallness of my mouth has always bothered me, but some people find it cute, even appealing, which totally surprises me.
–hoohoodini

the only problem that i have with my lips is that they get wicked chapped.
–cbgbgrl

LIPS AROUND THE WORLD

Lip adornments range from studs in the tongue or lower lip to huge, plate-size lip plugs found among Surma women in Ethiopia. When a young Surma woman first has her lips pierced, a small, coin-size disk is inserted into the hole. Over several years the size of the disk is increased, until it is 6 inches or so across, limiting both facial expression and speech. Elaborate lip ornaments were once found not only among various African peoples, but also in the Americas. Until the mid-1800s, for young Tlingit girls on the Northwest Coast of Alaska and Canada, acquiring a labret, or lip plug ornament, was a rite of passage marking her sexual maturation and indicating that she was ready for marriage. During the 19th century the fashion for European American women was a small, puckered, "beestung" mouth. To get that look, girls recited a series of words beginning with the letter "p."

LIP LOOKS

Women have been artificially reddening their lips for over 4,000 years, originally using red ochre for this effect. In modern times, lipstick rules—and different lip colors go in and out of fashion.

PURE RED - 1940s

BRIGHT PINK or CORAL - 1950s

PALE - 1960s

GLOSSY - 1970s

BLOOD RED or VAMPIRE BLACK - 1990s
Lip coloring can be used to create illusions. Pale colors tend to make thin lips look fuller, while darker shades have a slimming effect.

The full-lip look, long an African American ideal, became fashionable in the 1990s. Some women (including many white celebrities) began going to the extreme of getting collagen implants to achieve artificially inflated lips.

cupid's bow

full mouth

geisha

Cold Sores

Cold sores or fever blisters appear around the mouth and can be a real source of angst and embarrassment. The sores are caused by the herpes simplex 1 virus (related to the virus that causes genital herpes). They will heal untreated within a week or two, but there are also plenty of over-the-counter topical remedies that can speed healing. The amino acid lysine is a common alternative remedy. Your doctor can also prescribe medication. Cold sores are very contagious so it's important to avoid mouth contact or sharing lipstick with others. And do not touch the sore, which can easily spread to other parts of your body.

teeth

There are 32 teeth in a full adult grin, but teens may have only 28, as the four so-called wisdom teeth may not come in until sometime in the twenties (or they may never come in).

TEETH AROUND THE WORLD

While Western culture emphasizes straight, even, pearly white teeth, that is not a worldwide standard. Natchez and Choctaw Native American peoples traditionally blackened their teeth for beauty, as do Akha women today in the hills of Southeast Asia. Tooth filing and turquoise, gold, and other inlays were common among ancient peoples in Central America; anthropologists have identified almost 60 different kinds of tooth "improvements" there. Ancient Sudanese people removed or chipped their front teeth to achieve the beauty ideal. Braces date back to at least 700 BC, when they were worn by Etruscan girls.

Tooth Whiteness

The ideal of the extreme, super-white teeth has spawned a bunch of tooth-whitening products. In reality, it is absolutely natural to have teeth that are off-white. Some people are born without tooth enamel, which is what gives teeth their pearly color.

In addition to "whitening" toothpastes, there are several products that can be applied to the teeth for a more dramatic whitening effect. On the most expensive end of the spectrum, some people go to dentists for extensive tooth-bleaching treatments that involve the creation of a mold that is worn at night over three to four weeks. Do-it-yourself versions (available in drugstores) come with strips to be applied to the teeth over the course of a few weeks. These products and procedures all use peroxide, must be used with extreme caution, and can be harmful to tooth enamel in the end.

my lips are cool, but i hate my teeth. i'm getting them bleached, then i'll be fine.
—mangojam

I love my mouth! I have big lips that look gorgeous when I put on lip gloss. I have braces, but my teeth are really nice. I hate having braces though, cause I feel like a dork. I can't wait till I get them off!
—helovesme

I used to have buck teeth, but thank god for braces, now i have a beautiful smile.
—notalady

BRACES

About 70 percent of U.S. teenagers get braces. Most kids get them at the age of 11 or 12 (girls start before boys) and wear them for two to two and a half years. Braces are almost a rite of passage among preadolescent and adolescent girls. They are used to realign and straighten teeth, as well as to correct an overbite. In some cases, they are necessary for mouth health—for example, someone might have a couple of teeth removed and wear braces to "unpack" an overcrowded mouth, allowing the remaining teeth to establish strong roots—or to correct an underbite or overbite.

I have a gap in between my two front teeth, but I like it. My dentist said that it would go away once I got braces, but I don't really want the little gap to go away.
—so.hott

neck and shoulders

The neck contains the top seven vertebrae of the spine and plays a vital role in keeping us straight with heads held high—a universally appealing posture that symbolizes health, dignity, and power.

I think the neck is the most romantic place your boyfriend can kiss you. Like when he licks you and then blows on your neck, you say "oh, yeah."
–punkrockmaven

THE NECK IS A PRIME SPOT FOR BEAUTY MARKS AND MOLES. FOR MORE INFO, SEE PAGE 79.

argh, i've got a short, stubby neck!
–shorty02

I really like my neck. I don't have many "really great" features. But my neck is long and just nice. I often wear chokers and people actually compliment me!
–destinee

NECKLACES

The neck has been used for thousands of years as a place to show off symbols of power and wealth. Necklaces of shells and nuts have been found among the remains of prehistoric cave dwellers. In the past some people believed the soul resided in the base of the neck, so they placed a charm on a string around the neck to keep evil spirits away. Today, necklaces are worn primarily as decoration, although sometimes a special charm is put on for good luck or a symbol is worn as a sign of religious faith (like the cross). Types of necklaces may distinguish a particular fashion style (from old-fashioned cameo pendants to hippie beads to ultra-flashy gold) or an ethnic group. In Kenya, for example, on special occasions Samburu girls pile strands of beads in a tower from their shoulders to their chins.

NECKS AND SHOULDERS
AROUND THE WORLD

Women tend to have longer, more slender necks than men, and this difference is emphasized in the beauty ideal of a graceful, swanlike neck. All around the world, people have tried to emphasize the length of the neck.

Padaung women in Burma (Myanmar) and the Ndebele women of South Africa have taken the long-necked look to an extreme. At the age of five a Padaung girl has 5 brass rings placed around her neck and another is added each year, until she bears between 22 and 24 rings. These rings drastically weigh down the collarbones of the women, giving the shoulders a triangular slope and making the neck appear as long as 15 1/2 inches. The neck muscles are stretched and weakened by these neck ornaments, so if the rings are removed the neck may no longer fully support the head.

European women from the 16th through the 19th century wore corsets with shoulder straps that worked to push down the collarbone, thus making the neck appear longer (a device similar in function to the rings of the Ndebele).

Necks and Sexuality

In English, the term "necking" refers to kissing and caressing on a date. The neck is sometimes associated with a kind of sexual vulnerability, with the extreme example being the erotic vampire bite that results in death. Hickeys are red marks left on the neck (or other parts of the body) when a lover sucks the skin for a few seconds. They can take more than a day to fade away.

I have a long and slender neck, which some people joke makes me look like an ostrich.
–stylystarr80

EARS
AROUND THE WORLD

Some cultures have seen ears as the equivalents of a woman's geni-tals, and in ancient Egypt, if a woman cheated on her husband, her ears were cut off. In Asian cul-tures long ears were often believed to be a sign of wis-dom, and many Buddha sculp-tures have super-long ears. In other cultures—for instance, among the Dayak in Borneo—long ears are considered a sign of beauty, and young girls wear heavy brass earrings to stretch their lobes.

Ears are specially designed, with their curves and ridges, to gather sound. They are also very individual—no two people have the same ear pattern, so they're just as identifying as fingerprints.

EARRINGS

For more than 4,000 years people have worn earrings, whether as lucky charms, to protect against evil spirits, as signs of wealth, or as adornment. Sailors once believed that as long as they wore earrings they wouldn't drown at sea. In Africa, Maasai women in Kenya and Tanzania wore earrings as a sign of mar-riage, while Samburu women added beaded loops for each son who served as a warrior. In Japan, however, pierced ears were seen as harming the body and inviting bad luck.

BROAD SHOULDERS

Broad shoulders imply strength and have been a body ideal, more for men than for women, since the times of cave paint-ings (more than 25,000 years ago).

Broad shoulders can also be a sign of strength and athleticism. Swimmers, in particular, depend on upper-arm strength and have well-developed shoulder (and arm) muscles.

Neck and Shoulder Fashions

Japanese Samurai warriors (1600–1868) and Thai nobility (1350-1767) wore fashions that accentuated the shoulders with sculpted shapes ranging from boxy to pagoda-like curves.

In the late Middle Ages necklines were high and never showed the shoulders. People wore garments under their clothes (to protect from perspiration and staining) that peeked past the neckline and were gathered together into collars. By the 16th and 17th centuries this trend had evolved into the huge, circular collars known as ruffs.

Ruffs gradually became less stiffened, and the resulting "falling band" collars of the 17th and early 18th centuries mimicked the sloped-shouldered ideal of the time. The high collars of the late 19th century were in keeping with the pervading prudish Victorian attitudes.

In fact, for much of Western fashion history, women's shoulders have been covered, with the exception of low-cut evening gowns. All that changed in the 1920s, with the flapper era and its embrace of sleeveless fashions. However, certain religions and cultures still frown on so much display of the body, see-ing it as too immodest.

In 1937 the shoulder pad was introduced—the fashion ideal through the early 40s was a broad back and V-shaped body. The shoulder pad reemerged in the 80s as a part of the "power suits" that women wore to "dress-for-success."

back

The back is home to the all-important spinal column, which extends from your butt to your neck. From the rear view, the vertebrae that make up the spinal column usually line up fairly straight, but from the side they form a gentle S-curve.

My back is truly my favorite part of my body. I can't stop looking at the line my spine makes as it curves down the center!
—lillyah

I have scoliosis (my spine is curved) and my back hurts all the time!
—srahso

CURVY BACKS

Through poor posture, obesity, or some diseases, the spinal curve may become exaggerated. It can slouch forward with the top back in a hump (called kyphosis), or it can overarch, thrusting the butt and chest out (called lordosis). Scoliosis, a problem found in 10 percent of adolescent girls, is when the spine, looked at from behind, curves from side to side. Although a slight sideways curve in line with the dominant hand is normal, in scoliosis the curving is more pronounced, showing itself not only in the back but in off-kilter shoulder and hip levels as well as unevenly pronounced shoulder blades. Certain diseases may cause this condition, but most often it is thought to be something you are born with. No treatment is necessary unless the curving is more than 20 degrees off of your back's center line. Then you may need to wear a brace for a while and do back- and stomach-strengthening exercises to keep the back from curving even more. In severe cases, corrective surgery may be necessary. Treatment is important in helping prevent serious back problems later.

my back has a nice arch because i'm a gymnast and i work out.
—maeveC

I've been a competitive swimmer for almost 6 years now and it's done great things for my back and shoulder muscles...
—pandamania

BACK LOOKS

Painters like Velázquez in the 1650s knew that the sight of a soft, fleshy nude back could be just as alluring as a frontal view. More recently, in the 1930s, low-backed evening gowns became the rage, focusing attention on rear-view glamour and hinting at a state of undress. During competitions, bodybuilders pose in a back view, showing the strength of their taut trapezius (upper back) muscles. The Japanese, in particular, have revered the beauty of the back. Some of the most elaborate tattoos were painted on the canvas of geishas' backs.

While people have generally found straight backs appealing, this has not always been the case. In turn-of-the-20th-century France, an S-shaped spine was the ideal. The extreme, unhealthy corsets of the time actually molded the shape of the spine and altered women's posture.

SEE PAGE 25 FOR MORE ON CORSETS

BACK STRESS

The back is a very common point of tension in the body. If you feel stressed out or if you've been sitting down for long periods in front of the computer or the TV, you may feel it in your back. Just getting up and stretching every 15 minutes or so can help. Walking and swimming are great back exercisers. Practicing yoga, which stretches and strengthens the back, is good for overall health, can help cast off back tension, and may even offer relief for back problems like scoliosis. Back rubs and massages are always good back soothers.

SEE PAGE 42 FOR MORE ON YOGA

Other Back Issues

The back is a well-known and annoying place for acne to develop. In addition, some people grow thick hair on the lower back.

SEE PAGE 77 FOR MORE ON DEALING WITH ACNE. AND SEE PAGES 80–83 FOR MORE ON BODY HAIR.

i had a curvature of the spine. it showed up when I was 13. I couldn't even go to the beach because i was embarrassed that people would notice. 2 years ago i had surgery to correct the curve. Since then I feel more confident. i actually wear clothes that fit me.
—guruji

I hurt my back after college. I never had injuries before that and it really freaked me out. I worried that my back would never get better. Iyengar yoga has helped me a lot.
—silvergirlie

two words for you: BACK FLAB. i have love handles and i hate them.
—sweet.p

I hate it when you look good from the front and you turn around and there are blobs of back fat protruding from the seams of your bra.
—lol2002

i don't like my back very much because it is covered in acne and i don't know what to do about it.
—kobesgirl

I like the little bit of peach fuzz that I have on the small of my back.
—floral

well, i'm almost full-blooded italian and all italians are kinda hairy. every time i wear low-cut jeans or a low-cut shirt you can see my hairy back so now ppl call me wolfy.
—starprincess77

boobs

Boobs are a huge focus of attention in our society.

Much of that has do with their meaning: they are the most visible female sex organs, and they are the first source of human food. Whether you like it or not, your boobs (and everyone else's) are powerful symbols of sexuality and fertility.

Boobs are basically cushions of fat that surround the mammary glands (which produce milk after a baby is born). They come in all shapes and sizes—large, small, soft, firm, ball-like, tubelike, high, low, pointy, flat—mostly determined by heredity. There are often subtle size or shape differences between your two breasts. In most cases, the disparity is much less noticeable to anyone's eyes other than your own.

People have a lot of strong feelings about what makes boobs beautiful. As with everything else about appearance, different people are attracted to different kinds of breasts. In general, people tend to think that boobs are pretty great, whatever the particulars may be.

BOOBS
AROUND THE WORLD

Sculptors in ancient Greece rendered beautiful women with smaller breasts, believing the smallness of such a distinctive feature made it even more beautiful. Many cultures place less sexual emphasis on breasts than the U.S. does. In Europe, topless sunbathing is the norm, and bare breasts appear regularly in fashion magazines and advertisements. In some African tribes, parents massage and bind their daughters' breasts to make sure their nipples will be prominent.

BOOB SIZE AND SHAPE

Boob growth is one of the most noticeable changes that the body goes through. And there's no precise timetable for how they develop. During puberty, breasts grow at different rates. Sometimes they pop up, filling out within a few months; more often it's a gradual process, taking several years. It's often hard to predict exactly how they'll look in the end. It can take time for you (and the people around you) to get used to your boobs, especially if they sprout dramatically or early.

An increase in the hormone estrogen sparks breast growth, triggering the growth of the mammary glands and cushions of fat to surround these glands. Much of the volume of the breast comes from these cushions of fat.

Usually the first thing that's noticeable when breasts are coming in is that the nipple and the areola (the skin around the nipple) get larger and sometimes darker. The breasts continue to fill out and grow until they reach full size, which usually happens around age 17 or 18 or even later. Mostly, the final breast size is set by heredity, but hormonal changes (from birth control pills, pregnancy, or the menstrual cycle), as well as major weight loss or gain, can alter this size.

> I like my boobs. They are a 36D. Sometimes they are a pain in the butt, like when I play sports, I'm the only female there with three sports bras on. But I wouldn't trade them in for the world, they are my two "breast" friends.
> —jesse97

> I love my boobs. I'm only a size 34A, but I couldn't be happier, they're just enough for a handful, I don't have to think twice about going braless or wearing little tank tops, and they'll be perky forever! =) I wouldn't change them for anything!
> —snwbrdgrl

> Well, I wear a 36B and I feel like I am really small. I have wished for my boobs to grow bigger, but you can't speed up Mother Nature! My b/f told me it's not the boobs that really matter, it's what's behind the boobs that matters, my heart! Corny, but sweet and true!
> —dramababy00

> I have always wanted round, healthy-looking boobs, but you could poke an eye out with these things!
> —mykidd

> Every day in school someone walks up to me and says, "You have big boobs." I don't need someone to tell me how big they are because I know that already, idiot!
> —black_raven

bazongas ta-tas boobies hooters knockers

NIPPLES AND AREOLAS

Like breasts, nipples and areolas (the surrounding area) come in all shapes and sizes. The color of the areola may be pinker or browner, depending on heredity and skin tone. Nipples are generally sensitive to outside stimuli, becoming erect when touched or exposed to cold. In the 1930s film star Jean Harlow supposedly rubbed her breasts and nipples with ice before a shoot so her boobs would look extra-firm and her nipples would pop out. Usually nipples stick out, though it's not uncommon for them to be inverted, appearing to stick in. And sometimes they go from "innies" to "outies" during the course of development. But if there's any sudden change after your breasts fully develop, report it to your doctor.

Other Boob Issues

Stretch marks often appear on breasts that grow too fast for the skin to keep up. They usually fade with time. Some girls grow dark hair near their nipples.

More than 180,000 women are diagnosed with breast cancer each year. In some cases, a woman might face the possible removal of (a part or all of) one or both breasts. In addition to the serious health concerns, this can have a dramatic effect on body image.

My boobs are normal except for this weird thing with my nipples. They are really small, like the size of peas, and when they are not erect, they are all flat, they become like part of the dark circle around the nipple. They look really weird!
—glitteriegirl

i have an "innie" nipple. i'm fine w/it and so are the select few guys who've seen it!
—gothprincess

Don't worry about your nipples showing through your shirt when you're cold. It happens to all girls and there is no way to prevent it. Just cover em or when no one's looking push em back in lol. If your friends make fun of it say, "It's a bit nipply outside."
—lilspecial_kim

My left boob has an inverted nipple and I am embarrassed about it. I don't like getting into relationships that move fast because I'm afraid that if the guy finds out I have an inverted nipple, he will tell his friends about it and break up with me because I am a freak.
—ponpongirl

I am Super flat...I love my personality and the rest of my body, but when I look in the mirror all that seems to stand out on me is my FLAT GOOD-FOR-NOTHING chest. I wear a padded push-up bra, but in pool class I feel like a flat board and am so scared to show the real me off. I am afraid to "do stuff" with guys because I feel like when they take off my bra and see how flat I am, they'll make fun of me and tell all the guys in the world about my flat chest!
—shortie192

BOOB LOOKS

In the West, fashions in boobs have gone through lots of changes over the last 500 years, much of it having to do with the way corsets have been designed over time. In the 1500s the ideal for upper-class women was a smallish bust. Big boobs with deep cleavage were associated with the lower classes and wet nurses. By the 1600s this bustier look became the ideal. In the 1700s the ideal reverted back to a small firm bust. In the early 1800s corsets started being made with supports for each breast independently, which brought the separated breast into fashion. The monobosom was back at the beginning of the 20th century. The flapper look of the 1920s idealized a straight, flat chest, achieved in many cases by wearing bandeau bras that bound and suppressed the breasts.

The brassiere, originally made out of two handkerchiefs and some ribbon, was patented in 1914. In the 1930s the introduction of new elastic materials prompted experimentation with more structured support. Beginning in the late 1940s and up until the mid-1960s, cone-shaped bras, which lifted the breasts and pushed them together, became the norm—and cone-shaped breasts were the ideal. In the 60s, a more natural ideal emerged, sometimes braless, with lighter materials explicitly revealing the nipple in many cases. The 80s and 90s saw a return of the large-breasted, deep-cleavaged ideal, with padded bras, Wonderbras, and Water Bras playing supporting roles. Women also use breast enhancers, padding that goes on the outside of the breasts, to create the illusion of a larger silhouette.

Now there are bras to suit and shift every shape and size, whether you want to push up, pad, or minimize. Some women take the more serious step of having breast reduction or breast implant surgery.

SEE PAGE 91 FOR MORE ON BREAST SURGERY

FOR INFO ON STRETCHMARKS, SEE PAGE 79. FOR MORE ON BODY HAIR, SEE PAGES 80–83.

titties torpedos jugs melons honkers

arms and hands

ARM LOOKS

Naturally soft and fleshy arms were historically the ideal in Western culture as they signaled a woman of leisure who did not have to use her body to work. In recent times the rise of women's sports and America's fitness consciousness have created a desire for harder, more toned arms.

Arm muscles

The main arm muscles are the deltoids at the shoulders, which are used to raise the arm; the biceps on the front upper arm, used to bend the arm; and the triceps at the back of the upper arm, used to let the forearm reach out. In the natural course of things, everybody uses these muscles. Girls who are active generally have more developed muscles. Certain sports and exercise—swimming, rock climbing, gymnastics, and weight lifting, for example—have a more direct impact on building and toning arm muscles. But even carrying heavy things on a regular basis has an effect. Some girls lift weights with the sole intention of working out their arm muscles, because they want "toned" arms. While some girls like the look and feel of rippling muscles, others find them too "manly."

ARMPITS

Underarm hair begins growing usually sometime after pubic hair and boobs appear. This is when the underarm begins producing the pheromones that serve as sexual attractors. Underarm hair traps this scent and strengthens it.

The armpit is one of the major places on the body to produce sweat, the body's natural way of cleansing and cooling itself down. Odor often goes along with sweat, as bacteria accumulate on clothes and in warm, wet places.

My arms have always been really muscular, and I've always hated them. People tend to make fun of me for them, because "girls shouldn't be made of muscle," or something like that. Now, I just think that they're a part of me, and being strong is something I should be proud of, not ashamed.
–bounciebabe

We use our arms and hands constantly: eating, drinking, gesturing, writing, typing, opening doors, grooming ourselves, carrying stuff, and so much more.

I have toothpick arms. They're skinny and I can't wear tank tops without looking anorexic! I lift weights, do pushups, anything I can, and I still have stick arms!
–genesisgrl

The way your arms look has a lot to do with heredity. Arms can be naturally skinny, fleshy, or muscular. Muscle development, through regular activity or exercise, affects how strong your arms are as well as how they look.

i love my arms! i used to be a gymnast so they are very strong. even though sometimes shirts fit me funny, my arms make me feel strong and powerful! and sexy!
–lilcutey

i've always been overweight, and my arms only make it worse. they're fat, short, and make me look more horrible than i already look. but i've learned to wear loosearmed shirts so they look alright now.
–bubalababe

MANY GIRLS HAVE DARK, THICK ARM HAIR. FOR MORE ON BODY HAIR, SEE PAGES 80–83.

My arms are big b/c I am a gymnast. My whole upper body is muscular and it makes me feel very nonfeminine and makes me not want to wear cute stringy shirts.
–saffirebluemoon

My underarms sweat a lot—I mean A LOT!
–troubled02

HANDS

A person is likely to bend and stretch her hands some 25 million times during her life. Besides their utilitarian functions, hands are remarkably expressive. Sign language is based on the expressiveness of hands, as is much of Asian dance. Thai dancers put on elongated finger ornaments to enhance this expressive potential.

Historically, the appearance of a person's hands provided a clue to her social status. Soft, untanned skin and long, well-manicured nails marked the hands of a "lady" who didn't have to work in the house or the fields. Gloves were an absolute fashion necessity for upper-class European women, shielding hands from the sun. While hands are no longer a reflection of social status, a pianist's long fingers or paint under an artist's nails might offer clues about a person.

ARM AND HAND ADORNMENT

Decoration can enhance beautiful arms and hands, or even call attention away from features you don't find attractive.

Hand decoration

Mehndi is the Indian name for a popular technique in the Middle East, India, and North Africa for painting hands and feet with designs in henna, a natural dye, which may range in color from orange to red to a deep brown. The technique was first used thousands of years ago in Egypt. Today, designs vary from decorative floral patterns to fertility symbols. The art has gained popularity in the U.S. Applying a mehndi design takes up to several hours and may last for two weeks to a month.

Rings

Both men and women have been wearing rings for 4,000 years or more. Sometimes they were worn for magical protection, sometimes as a sign of allegiance to a particular person (the wedding ring is a variation of this). The tradition of wearing wedding and engagement rings on the fourth finger (counting from the thumb) came from the idea that a special nerve or vein ran from that finger to the heart. At times, rings were an indication of social status. Wealthy women in ancient Egypt wore as many as three rings on a finger, and in Europe during the 1700s elaborately jeweled rings might cover every joint on a well-to-do woman's hands.

Bracelets

Since prehistoric times, women around the world have worn bracelets. In ancient Greece, women wore snakelike bracelets with their sleeveless togas, but aristocratic medieval women only occasionally wore bracelets, preferring to cover their arms with ornately embroidered designs. In India women don wedding bracelets, consisting of multiple bangles, while in Ethiopia Hamar women adorn their arms with a series of iron coils.

Nail looks

Women have been decorating their nails for thousands of years. As far back as 3000 BC, Egyptian women used henna to color their nails. And in the Ming dynasty (1368–1644), Chinese women glossed their nails with a mixture of beeswax, gum arabic, and egg whites. The type of polish in use today was developed from auto-body paint in the early 20th century. (Check for toluene- and formaldehyde-free brands, as these chemicals can be hazardous to health.)

In addition to polish, girls decorate their nails with decals, nail jewels, and fake nails, creating varied looks and styles. Long nails can be easily achieved with fake nails, though the adhesives used on these nails can damage your real nails, especially if you leave them on for more than three days.

A generally healthy diet and moisturizing hand cream in the dry winter months should ensure healthy nail growth and solid, attractive nails. Lots of girls bite or pick their nails, especially when they're under stress. People try different techniques to stop this—like polishing their nails with super-bitter stuff or paying for manicures—with varying degrees of success.

belly and hips

The belly serves the important function of protecting your internal reproductive organs—your ovaries, fallopian tubes, and uterus. Biologically, this accounts for the extra cushioning of fat often found there. Additionally, women's bellies are ready and able to accommodate the extended uterus (and growing fetus) of pregnancy.

The widening of the hips, one of the body changes that occurs during puberty, also happens in preparation for childbirth. The cushioned belly, hips, and breasts—the hallmarks of female fertility—are what make girls curvier than guys.

BELLIES AND HIPS AROUND THE WORLD

African tribes worshipped fertility symbols with protruding stomachs as signs of health and abundance. And for hundreds of years, until the late 1600s, Europeans revered a full-looking belly. In a great many parts of the world where food is scarce, a fleshed-out stomach is still a desirable attribute.

Through much of history, broad, fleshy hips have been idealized as well. Starting from the 14th century, women's skirts exaggerated and accentuated hip lines with man-made supports like petticoats, cushions, and hoops. Many of these supports served to accentuate the butt as well.

The popularity of the corset in the 15th century created a smaller waist, which in turn accentuated the fullness of the hips (and the bust). In the 1920s there was a radical shift in style, with the straight-line silhouette becoming the fashionable ideal. Gradually, the hip line curved its way back into fashion, peaking after World War II. English and American 60s fashion idealized a more androgynous body type for models, which still exists today. While certain clothes may hang better on a straight silhouette, in real life and in many people's minds, curviness is a big part of sexiness. For African Americans and Latinas in particular, big hips are especially appreciated.

Sometimes i feel like my belly is great and it couldn't look hotter, but then i see all the propaganda put out by our shallow media and i wish i could trade it in for a new and improved model (preferably from a model).
—outtasitechic

SEE PAGE 25 FOR MORE ON HOW THE CORSET CHANGED THE BODY'S SILHOUETTE

BELLY SIZE

Low-rise fashions put a lot of extra emphasis on the belly and consequently make a lot of people extremely self-conscious about the natural size of their bellies. Stomachs, like everything else, come in different shapes and sizes. Bellies have become something of a focal point for weight-obsessed girls, who often end up comparing themselves to an exaggerated, gym-created ideal.

I have this pudge on my stomach, which I am sure most girls have. I used to complain and cry about it, but my boyfriend loves it and he lets me know all the time.
—doodlenoodle

My belly is usually fit, firm, and tight during swim season.
—tall_sally

I used to not like my belly and some-times I still don't like the way some pants make it look. But recently I got my belly button pierced and now I want to show it off.
—surferchic82

i have an outie. all my friends think it's nasty, but it's different and my boyfriend loves playing with it. i love it!
—citypretty

my friends informed me that my belly button looks like an innie that threw up. At first i was a little per-turbed...but now i love my button. it's a great conversation starter.
—katieT

belly buttons are so underappreciated! love your belly button in every way, may it be hairy, pierced, innie, outie, whatever! it was once your source of life, ja know....
—supagirl19

my stomach is probably my worst feature. i'm not fat or any-thing, it's just not flat. every magazine i look at has all those models with those perfect flat stomachs, and i always wish i had a flat stomach.
—maybeebaby

A lot of girls are worried about their hips and butts being too big. Well, frankly, I wish I had more of both. Sometimes it feels like I have no curves, and I am very self-conscious about it, especially when I wear tight jeans. If I could change something about my body, it would definitely be to have curvy, thick hips.
—starblazer

All of my friends have really big hips. But me nooo, I had to be the oddball, my hips are so straight, ya know those hip-hugger jeans? Well, I can't wear em cause I have no hips to hug!
—crazykookie

I love my hips. They make me look more voluptuous.
—moulinred

My hips are a lil wide and I think I look fat. My friends tell me looks fine. I asked a bunch of guys what they think about big hips and they said they think it's sexy. Now I am happy to have big hips.
—volleyballbabe

While other girls my age are getting boobs, guess what? I'm getting hips! I have a 26" waist, and 37" hips. It's crazy! The good thing is, they're probably my best weapon. All I need to do is bump someone and they go flying!
—msthangtoo

BELLY BUTTONS

Belly buttons can be innie, outie, or in between. There is no right kind of belly button to have. Navel-exposing styles have drawn a lot of attention to the once-hidden belly button and have surely contributed to the recent increase in belly button piercings. But it wasn't so long ago that belly buttons were deemed unaccept-able for public viewing. In the 1970s, for example, Cher came in for heavy criticism when she exposed hers on TV.

Belly and Hip Issues

Scars, moles, and birthmarks show up on lots of girls' bellies. Stretch marks, which occur anywhere that the body grows faster than the skin, are com-mon on the hips and belly. Belly-baring styles have made girls self-conscious about belly hair.

FOR MORE INFO ON BIRTH-MARKS AND STRETCH MARKS, SEE PAGE 79. FOR MORE ON BODY HAIR, SEE PAGES 80–83.

crotch

The crotch is an area of the body that many people have trouble talking about. The way girls and women feel about this area can affect the way they feel about their sexuality and their self-image in general.

This is probably why the crotch can generate extreme feelings: Some women believe it is the most beautiful part of the body, a source of sexual pleasure and something to be celebrated. Others, who may have been taught that this area of their bodies is shameful and dirty, may extend that feeling to the rest of themselves. Many women have less intense feelings, or focus in on a particular aspect of the crotch.

WHAT'S UP DOWN THERE?

The crotch consists of the vulva—the outer genitals—and any pubic hair surrounding it. Everybody's vulva is unique and varies in color, shape, and size. Getting to know what your own vulva looks like (you can do this by holding a mirror between your legs) can help to make the area less mysterious and more real.

> I hate having pubic hair!!!!! It gets in the way. And when you have to shave your bikini line it itches so freaking bad!!!!! And sometimes you get these little red bumps!! Am I the only one with these problems?!?!?!?
> —loudbb

> I hate how bathing suit companies don't take into consideration that we have hair on our crotches! It makes buying swimsuits very difficult and time-consuming...
> —BeeBaby

> well, i always thought i had an abnormal crotch because my inner lips they hung down farther than i thought they were supposed to. well, then i got to talking to my cousin about it and she said hers were the same way. it gave me a lot of relief.
> —candylope

> I guess my crotch is ok–it's not a hindrance, let's put it that way! But people talk about shaving and I'm not for that, so I just trim every now and then with scissors. My boyfriend is a little happier when I do that!
> —Zoolandia

> I think that my crotch needs more hair because I have the least pubic hair in my class.
> —singababe

PUBIC HAIR

Pubic hair starts growing around the same time your boobs appear and your period begins. Every girl has her own growth pattern, much of it influenced by heredity. Pubic hair generally grows in phases, starting out thin and centralized and eventually forming a bushy patch. According to scientists, pubic hair helps to protect the sensitive genital area from dirt and other irritants.

Bathing suit fashions, in particular, make the bikini line a cause of concern for many American girls, who are embarrassed by the public display of their pubic hair. (European girls and women seem to be much less bothered by this.)

Whether to do anything about the hair that covers the vulva itself— trim, shave, wax, use depilatory, et cetera—is another issue that gets talked about a lot in the context of being sexually intimate with another person. There is no right way to handle this. Some women leave it alone, some trim it, some remove most of the hair but leave a thin strip (called a Brazilian wax), and some choose to remove all the hair. Guys have differing opinions about it as well. It is important to keep in mind that the skin on the vulva is extra-sensitive so any hair removal there should be done with caution!

> well, um, this is kinda embarrassing, but i wanna know if guys like it hairy or shaved...i think i should shave but when i tried, it kinda hurt. but i want my boyfriend to be happy.
> —Purplehaze

FOR MORE INFO ON BODY HAIR, SEE PAGES 80–83

it's weird. i mean i love having one for pleasure reasons but it smells kinda funny...
—poser_girl

It does what it's supposed to do, but I don't know how any guy could ever want to go down there... It's really gross. Hairy. Ick.
—sweet_tea

CROTCHES AROUND THE WORLD

Throughout Africa and in some Middle Eastern countries, parents massage infant daughters' genitals to make their labia lips hang down because that is considered attractive.

In many tribes throughout rural Africa, adolescent girls are forced to undergo clitorectomies (removal of the clitoris). Movements are under way to put an end to this sort of genital mutilation.

I really like my vagina. I love the musk odor...
—artluvr17

well, does anyone ever think that when you're ready to have sex, he'll think it's ugly?
—HickoryNut

I felt like - who would want to go down there with all that hair and stuff? My boyfriend doesn't really care, he just wants to make me feel good.
—scarlet

I feel that it's my sexiest part. There's not any reason why, i just think that it's nice and HAIRY. I find that very appealing.
—wassabie

It makes me feel dirty and embarrassed. I wish it was less hairy and just different in some way. It makes me feel uneasy.
—onthedl

THE CROTCH AND SEXUALITY

Feeling dirty or shameful about your crotch can have a negative impact on any sexually intimate relations you may have. Feeling ashamed about your crotch—its odor, hair, lips, discharge—can stop you from being able to fully enjoy your sexuality.

Vaginal Odor

Vaginal odor is a natural part of having a vagina and is actually part of the vagina's function. Pheromones (sexual attractors) in the vaginal fluid serve to arouse sexual interest. And pubic hair is thought to make the scent of pheromones easier to smell. (Medieval knights wore a lock of their lady's pubic hair as a good-luck charm in battle.)

Vaginal odor changes with your menstrual cycle and should generally be inoffensive. If you notice a particularly strong odor, look for other symptoms of infection, and call a doctor if you think there may be a problem.

Chastity Belts

During the Middle Ages, to guard against any display of sexual freedom, European women were expected to wear "chastity belts." Made of heavy material or sometimes even metal, these devices, locked in place, encased the crotch and whole pelvic area. According to legend, these belts were first worn by the wives of knights who rode off to fight the Crusades. Only the husband held the key to his wife's belt.

butt

Butts are an endless source of fascination for the human species. The gluteus maximus, as it is officially known, is the strongest muscle in the body. Besides being the primary means by which we sit down and stand up, the butt has a number of clear biological purposes. Our backsides are padded to keep us from hurting our sensitive spots when we sit or fall down. The butt is also the home of the anus, which is the entry to the rectum and the exit point of fecal matter (otherwise known as poop, among other nastier names). As a result, some people associate the butt with dirtiness. This concept of the butt as "bad" is reinforced by the idea of spanking as punishment.

The butt is the next-door neighbor of the genital area for both sexes—it is probably a combination of these two factors that makes the butt part of our sexual allure. For some people, this extends to making the butt the primary sexual object (as in anal sex). For others, it just means they find butts attractive. Humans are far from the only species to focus on the butt as a sexual place—some primate females develop swellings on their rears to demonstrate their fertility.

Because butts figure into sexual attraction, there are lots of strong opinions about what an ideal butt should be. It's the distribution of muscles and fat on the butt that creates so much variation in shape, size, and firmness. Attitudes about what makes a good butt vary from culture to culture (and person to person). Some girls enjoy the attention butts tend to attract, while others would rather do without it.

I have some fine ass! It's really big! I love that song "I like big butts..." because it gives me confidence! Be proud of that ass! SHAKE WHAT YOUR MAMA GAVE YOU!
–downsouthie

Being a teen girl and seeing all the videos with big bootie girls I feel very self-conscious because my butt is rather small.
–Iamthewalrus

BUTTS AROUND THE WORLD

In many places around the world, particularly in African and Latin American cultures, round, full buttocks are considered beautiful. In southern Africa, for instance, Khoikhoi and San women are complimented for fleshy behinds. In Senegal, in western Africa, girls may add padding to their derrieres to get the desired fuller look. Italian men pinch women's butts in several different ways: pizzicato (brief), vivace (forceful with several fingers), and sostenuto (for a sustained period of time, while rotating).

Me and my friends used to argue over which kind guys like more - big butts or little butts. I have a little butt, so I argued that point, saying they were cute. Some of my friends don't care what kind of butt I have, or if guys like it, because I argued that guys like big butts because... well, they're big. Personally, I don't think they should be judging me on my butt anyway!
–bubbliscious1

fanny
bootie
rear end

buns tail heinie

BUTT LOOKS

For much of history, big, well-rounded, soft derrieres were a beauty ideal, and often they still are. Bustles—padding worn underneath women's skirts that accentuated the butt—were worn by fashionable Western women starting in the late 1700s.

Today, fake fannies are consistently one of the top-selling items of lingerie giant Frederick's of Hollywood.

Beginning in the 1920s, the flapper era, the slim look took hold. By the 1950s the girdle was keeping fleshy, jiggly butts in check. Although girdles lost their grip in the 1970s, the emphasis on butt control continued. Super-snug designer jeans may show off the rear, but they also keep it within strict bounds. With the fitness frenzy of the 1980s, butt shaping (toning the gluteus muscle) really took off. The workout tape "Buns of Steel" sold over 13 million copies.

The rise of hip-hop culture at the end of the 20th century—with songs like "Baby Got Back"— has helped to re-elevate the beauty of the big butt in the U.S., as has the popularity of Latina star Jennifer Lopez.

I'm a latina but I have no butt. All the women in my family have butts like J.Lo or bigger and I have nothing.
–prettylilflower

i have a voluptuous body with wide hips and definite junk in the trunk. i sometimes look at skinny models and wonder why my butt isn't as small as theirs.
–bestfriend4ever

my butt has always been small. i love it, and i buy pants that show it off!
–hannAhAh

I don't exactly hate my butt, but I don't love it either. It's just THERE.
–chocoyoga

I like my butt. It has character. It comes in handy too...have you ever seen a person with a small butt open a door with it?
–hiphophunn

I HATE MY BUTT!!! every time i walk anywhere, my big butt is tagging along for the ride. guys are always looking and whistling...i hate feeling like a piece of meat. it's hard to shop for pants too because you have to buy at least 1-2 sizes bigger than what you are, and it makes me look fatter.
–frenchfries13

i am black and usually black women have big hips and bootie. but i got a little bootie. sometimes it makes me feel depressed...
–flipfloppin

tuchas
behind
derriere
caboose
rump **backside**
buttocks **tush**
bum **tushy**

legs

Legs keep us upright, move us around, and carry us from place to place. Leg length often depends on body height, as legs usually account for about half the body height. Growth spurts can sometimes make them look long and gangly, but proportions usually even out. Legs (along with boobs and butts) are often seen as symbols of sexiness, probably because of what's between them.

LEG LOOKS

For hundreds of years, legs were not a fashion issue. Women's legs were out of sight in much of the world, hidden beneath long skirts or other floor-length garments. Legs first started getting a bit of attention in the United States with the bicycle-riding craze of the late 19th century, although long skirts were still the norm. It was only during the 1920s that flappers rebelled against this standard and started wearing shorter skirts that exposed their lower legs and even their knees. Dances like the Charleston became all the rage, with women showing off their high-stepping legs. Thighs, however, remained covered up—except in pinup images of movie stars like Betty Grable, noted for her "gams." It wasn't until the 1960s, when miniskirts and bikinis gained favor, that thighs came decidedly into public view.

My legs are INSANE-LY long. I love em, but I hate em. After shopping at 5 malls, in 2 different cities, I am STILL looking for a pair of pants that touches the top of my shoes. But since they are long, they look good in skirts, shorts, or swimsuits.
—guitarstar

I love my legs, although I'm rather self-conscious about them. I've really built up my leg muscles in track, cross-country, and fencing. When I wear shorts, I've got a guy either impressed by my build or freaked out.
—pearlpule

I'm so short for my age that that it makes my legs look "stumpy."
—thili_sis

Nobody
is satisfied
with their thighs, I
can tell you that. If
you look closely you
usually find something
wrong. That's why i
don't pay attention to
them anymore. I just go
jogging about once or
twice a week to keep
my body in shape.
-myboyishot

Cellulite

Cellulite is the kind of dimply fat that appears naturally on 80 to 90 percent of women's upper legs, stomachs, or butts, whether or not they are overweight. By 1995 more than 100 million dollars was wasted each year on the false promises of "cellulite busters." Despite what the advertisements say, there's no scientific evidence that any cream can eliminate these fat cells.

Other Leg Issues

Legs can have various marks on them. They are a particularly popular place for scars to appear, especially for girls who play field sports or do other leg-centric activities.

Everyone has some hair on their legs. Many girls choose to remove theirs.

My thighs
are huge! I call
them thunder
thighs and my
friends and I
have even start-
ed our own lit-
tle club
because of it.
What can I say?
Once you get
over the fact of
having thighs that
could swallow a
whale, you deter-
mine that they
sure do give
you quite the
figure when in
a dress.
-tigerpower

THIGHS

Thighs, along with the hips and belly, often gain a cushion of fatty tissue at puberty in preparation for childbearing. They also house the quadriceps muscles, which are used to lift the upper leg and are some of the biggest muscles in the body. These two factors contribute to the thigh's relative thickness compared to the rest of the leg.

Since the rise of aerobics and the fitness culture in the 1980s, thighs (like the belly) have become something of a negative focus of weight-obsessed girls and women, who compare themselves to an often abnormally thin thigh standard.

FOR MORE ON SCARS, SEE PAGE 79.
FOR MORE ON BODY HAIR,
SEE PAGES 80–83.

LEGS
AROUND THE WORLD

In Brazil, Alto Xingu and Mato Grosso girls tightly bind their upper legs in an attempt to swell their thighs—considered a sign of beauty. And in Guyana, Wauwai girls bind their calves to produce a similar effect.

My legs
are all torn
up from
playing com-
petitive soft-
ball. I use knee
sliders but every
time I slide they
always come down
and I have a new
scar. My friends
told me my scars
are battle
wounds and to
be proud of
them, and I
am!
-sillysoup

feet

Your feet may be the most amazing part of your body. Leonardo da Vinci called them a "masterpiece of engineering and a work of art." Each foot contains 26 bones and 20 muscles, plus some 7,000 nerve endings that constantly sense the ground as we stand and tell our brains how to adjust our posture so we stay balanced.

FOOT SIZE AND SHAPE

Your feet are shaped by heredity. They can be naturally long, short, wide, thin, flat, arched—and the same goes for the toes. Generally speaking, the taller you are, the bigger feet you have, though there are many exceptions to this. Many girls have different-sized feet—66 percent of U.S. women have one foot that is bigger than the other, according to a study by the Women's Shoewear Council. Also, feet generally swell during the day, so what fits in the morning may not fit as comfortably in the evening. The average shoe size for American women is a size 8 wide, though interestingly the women's top-selling shoe size is a 7 1/2 medium. One survey showed that 88 percent of U.S. women wore shoes that were too small, though it is unclear why.

I have huge feet! My family says I have "boat feet" or "flippers." I used to hate it. The shoes I liked never came in my size, and if I did find shoes I liked, they made my feet look so big! I guess I just got over it. Anyways, they make me a better swimmer.
—thekangaroo

I have thong feet—my friends tease me because one next to it. It may look weird, but hey! They're designed specifically for flip-flops! There is a huge space between my big toe and the
—diamondintheruff

In general I think all feet are ugly, but I have to give them credit, you'd be ugly too if you had to walk around on your face all day!
—Jamsterhamster

my feet are cute but people make fun and call them flintstone feet cuz they are like little squares... oh well...Yaba-daba-dooooo!
—reignofdreams

FOOT LOOKS

AROUND THE WORLD

Feet have been dressed in and shaped by shoes for thousand of years, beginning with foot coverings made from plant leaves and animal skins. Shoe fashion has alternated between a square-, round-, or pointy-toed look. In the 1500s in Europe, the popular **poulaine** or **crakow** style had a pointed toe that extended four or more inches. Shoes have had lifted soles—from less than an inch to over twenty inches—for centuries. In the 16th century, women walked slowly through the muddy, flooded streets of Venice in platform **chopines**. The modern platform shoe, first introduced in the 1930s, had a revival in the early 1970s and is still popular today, especially among young Japanese women who wear platforms so high they can barely walk.

High-heeled shoes first appeared in the late 1500s, getting higher and lower, and going in and out of fashion ever since.

From the 1100s to the 1900s, the painful Chinese practice of footbinding resulted in 3- to 5- inch feet with a lotus-blossom shape.

FOR MORE ON HIGH HEELS, SEE PAGE 25

FOR MORE ON FOOT BINDING, SEE PAGE 89

FOR INFO ON NAIL POLISH, SEE PAGE 65

the backs of my heels are permanently red, along with my mauled toes. i do pointe (toe ballet), so that wreaks havoc on my feet and causes the skin to rub off and for me to get blisters, it hurts, but they let me do what i love. so as long as they're in dance shoes, they're beautiful!
  —spiderchick52

I have toenail fungus on a few of my toes. My toenails get thick and yucky. Sometimes I can cover it with polish but not always. It makes open-toed shoes a big issue for me, which sucks because I really like open-toed shoes! I find it repulsive and hideous and it's really hard to cure. :(
  —jadelous

Foot Wear and Tear

Feet come in for a lot of use and abuse. The average person takes about 9,000 to 10,000 steps every day. At that pace she is likely to walk around the world about four times during her life. How the feet actually look after all this walking depends a lot on the kind of shoes (if any) that are worn. Blisters, bunions, corns, and calluses are common problems caused by footwear that's too tight or pointy. Dancers (ballet dancers in particular) use their feet very strenuously, and their feet typically reflect this use.

Foot Fungus

Lots of girls, especially athletes, get fungus on their feet (athlete's foot), usually on the bottom and sides, as well as on the toes. Fungus appears as peeling, cracking, or scaly skin. It grows in damp places, including sweaty feet and feet that aren't dried well after swimming or bathing. Fungus can be treated with over-the-counter topical ointments. Toenail fungus, which may be spread by using unsterilized pedicure equipment, is also common.

Foot Odor

There are 250,000 sweat glands in the feet, which can make them pretty smelly—smelly enough to leave a scent that dogs can track even through shoes.

skin

Skin is the largest body organ. The average person carries around about six pounds of skin, or some 20 square feet. It contains nerves, sweat glands, sebaceous glands, and hair shafts. Healthy skin is elastic and strong and constantly renewing itself. It is coated by sebum, an oil that keeps skin smooth and flexible and protects it. Skin does its best to defend the body from bacteria and viruses. The thickest skin is on the soles of your feet; the thinnest on your eyelids.

SUN AND THE SKIN

Excessive exposure to the sun damages elastic tissue in the lower layer of the skin (the dermis), which leads to loss of skin tone and wrinkles, and can dry out your skin. Through ultraviolet radiation, the sun causes 1 million new cases of skin cancer a year, a disease that can be disfiguring and sometimes life-threatening. Even one bad sunburn can increase your chances of getting skin cancer. While fair-skinned people are the most vulnerable to sunburns, people of all skin colors can get skin cancer.

For most people, sun damage occurs before the age of 20—so if you are a teenager, you have a good opportunity to treat your skin right from the start.

At any age, it is important to be careful about sun exposure. When you are outside for any length of time, use sunscreen with a sun protection factor (SPF) of at least 15 that protects against both UVA and UVB ultraviolet radiation. If you are outside a lot or if you have fair skin, wear wide-brimmed hats that cover the nose, and tightly woven clothes to protect the rest of your body. People with especially fair skin might try to stay in the shade if possible during peak sun hours (10 am to 4 pm).

Wrinkles

Wrinkles around your eyes and mouth can form as early as your late teens. The number one cause of wrinkles is exposure to sun, though smoking also causes wrinkles around the mouth. In addition to sun block, which can prevent wrinkling, good moisturizers containing tretinoin ingredients (found in retinoid creams) or alpha-hydroxy acids are thought to help smooth out the appearance of fine lines.

My skin is really white. Yes, I am Irish. I don't tan at all. But I have learned to be grateful for my fair skin. My mom always tells me that I won't get old and wrinkled like people who tan. —pennylane99

my skin is a mixture of creamy caramel and milk chocolate. —raindancer7

I have pale skin but I am Hispanic. All my life I've been teased - they call me white girl. I can't stand it b/c I just don't fit in with the Hispanic women and African American women I hang with. —genesisgirl

My mom is white and my dad is black so I'm mixed and look mixed. People really love my skin color because they say I always look tan (cuz I am). It's great! —sek_c_bee

i have really dark skin. while everyone is lying out over the summer and frying their skin, i already have a tan year-round! —sugarmiss

SKIN COLOR

Skin color varies by ethnicity and comes from pigment cells in the epidermis (the top layer of your skin). These cells make a substance called melanin, which is a brownish black. The more cells there are and the more melanin they produce, the darker the skin. (Albinos have a lack of pigment in the skin, hair, and eyes and appear ultra-white.) The color of your skin is determined by your genes, although children can be significantly lighter or darker than their parents. There is a tremendous variety of skin tones.

Despite the overwhelming evidence that excessive exposure to the sun is damaging to the skin, the tan look remains extraordinarily popular—and girls often bemoan the fact that they are too pale. (This may be in part a result of the darkening average skin tone of our increasingly multicultural population.) People have been temporarily changing the color of their skin for thousands of years. This continues today with self-tanners, foundations, and bleachers.

FOR MORE ON SKIN, SEE PAGES 85

FOR INFO ON HOW PALE OR TANNED SKIN HAS GONE IN AND OUT OF FASHION, SEE PAGE 16

i used to get back zits a lot. i worried about them when i joined the swim team until a boy saw my embarrassment and removed his shirt. he showed me how bad his back was and we laughed. —dramarama18

I have this one wrinkle in the center of my brow. I really do think I am too young for such a deep wrinkle. It is so deep because I am in chronic pain. I hope someday to view it as a badge of honor, if I don't inject it with Botox first ;-) —unexplainableme

SKIN CARE

There are some basic things to do (and not do) to keep your skin healthy. Washing the skin gently with a mild cleanser will remove dirt and bacteria that can clog pores. Using harsh cleansers and too much water can cause drying or cracking. The skin is about 70 percent water, but some of that water is constantly evaporating into the air and needs to be replaced—so drinking lots of water is important. Too much alcohol, coffee, or caffeine may dehydrate your skin. Figuring out how to relieve stress, which can have negative effects on your skin, will also help keep it in good condition. Smoking prematurely ages the skin. And lack of sleep slows down the skin's natural healing process.

SKIN CARE THROUGH THE AGES

Throughout history, women have used a variety of products to improve their skin. Three thousand years ago, in ancient Egypt, women used perfumed oils as well as mixtures containing hippopotamus fat or crushed donkeys' teeth. In ancient Syria, camels' lungs were a skin-care ingredient. Wealthy ancient Greeks kept virginal female slaves on very strict diets so their urine and saliva would be pure enough to use in skin-softening creams. In ancient Rome, crocodile dung was prized for revitalizing facial masks, and upper-class women went to bed with fresh meat on their faces to soften their skin. During the late 14th century the future French queen, Isabel of Bavaria, washed her face with a concoction that included boar brains, wolf blood, and crocodile glands.

In the 19th century American women made skin treatments with ingredients like horseradish and sour milk. Urine is a skin-care ingredient mentioned in both North and Central American folklore, especially the "warm urine of a little boy." Young people in the Society and Austral islands (near Australia) bleach and soften their skin with leaf sap to make themselves more desirable to potential mates.

i just wish acne was never a part of ANYONE'S life. Everything would be much easier, no foundation, no acne medication, NO DERMATOLOGIST!!!
—freakyangel11

SKIN CONDITIONS

There are a number of common skin conditions that people find annoying or irritating.

Acne

Acne is the number one complaint people have about their skin. It generally makes its first appearance during adolescence, when androgen hormones start stimulating the sebaceous glands in your pores to make sebum—oil for your hair and skin. When too much oil is produced, pores can get clogged and then inflamed, causing acne. There are oil-producing glands all over the body, but the overactive ones are often concentrated in the T-zone on your face (across the forehead and down the nose and chin) and on the chest and back. So these are the areas where acne is most common.

More than anything, heredity will determine if you get acne and how severe it is, but hormones also play a role in the condition of your skin. Women often experience breakouts at certain times of their menstrual cycle, usually due to an increase in progesterone, a hormone that is produced after ovulation and before menstruation. Anxiety and stress are also known to trigger breakouts, as they cause the adrenal glands to release more androgens (another hormone).

There are a number of things you can do to manage acne. It always helps to practice good skin care. Beyond that, there are over-the-counter products that contain benzoyl peroxide or alpha-hydroxy acids that some people find helpful in controlling acne. Various products and ingredients have different effects on different people. If nothing seems to work for you, it's a good idea to see a dermatologist. She or he may prescribe antibiotics, retin-A cream, or the powerful anti-acne drug Accutane, which should never be taken if you are pregnant or think you might be.

It is not a good idea to touch, squeeze, pick at, or pop your pimples (even if it's very tempting). You can make them worse, drive them deeper, and leave small scars on your face.

FOR MORE ON TAKING CARE OF YOUR BODY, SEE PAGES 40–41

BLACKHEAD—when a pore gets clogged but stays open.

WHITEHEAD—when a pore gets bacteria in it that infects the oil gland and produces redness and whitish yellowish pus.

PIMPLE—when a clogged pore closes and protrudes from the skin.

Dry Skin

Dry skin is unhealthy, mostly because skin that is cracking or peeling is more likely to let in bacteria that would normally be blocked. Drinking lots of water is one of the most basic steps to take to keep your skin moisturized. Exposure to the sun can also dry out the skin, so practicing sun protection is an important preventive measure.

Cool wintertime air is especially drying, so using a humidifier goes a long way toward preventing skin dryness. Avoiding extremely hot water and too many soaps and detergents also helps. Moisturizers add moisture to the top layer of skin as well as protecting skin from the air.

Warts

Warts are caused by viruses. Most of them will go away by themselves, especially those that are less than a year old. If you're in a hurry, though, there are a number of effective over-the-counter treatments, as well as natural remedies, the most popular being vitamin E applied directly and often. Vitamin A is also recommended. Dermatologists treat warts by burning or freezing them off, though they tend to reappear in many cases.

Bumps or Keratosis Pilaris

Many girls and women complain about little reddish bumps, or "chicken skin," on their upper arms or thighs. These are caused by a condition known as keratosis pilaris. About 42 percent of the population is affected by this condition, which is more common in girls than boys. The bumps typically appear during the early teenage years and are more prevalent in winter. The bumps sometimes go away on their own. Doctors recommend wearing loose, nonitchy fabrics; taking lukewarm rather than hot showers; and using mild soaps and lotions. Alpha-hydroxy cream may work too.

Eczema

Eczema is a skin allergy that usually appears as red, flaky patches on the skin and may, at first, just seem like extra-dry skin. The trouble is, it doesn't go away. A dermatologist can prescribe medications or creams to treat it.

Psoriasis

Patches of irrritated, itchy, scaly skin, especially on the scalp, hands, elbows, knees, and feet, may be a sign of psoriasis. The problem is essentially an overactive skin, which makes new cells and pushes up old ones at an accelerated rate. A dermatologist can prescribe the best treatment.

SWEAT AND ODOR

Sweat is the body's natural way of cleansing and cooling itself down. Skin all over the body contains sweat glands, which are particularly active in the armpits, back, hands, feet, and vulva. Androgens stimulate these glands when the body exercises, overheats, or faces some kinds of stress. Hormonal levels also rise before your period, causing more sweat.

Bacteria grows in warm, wet places. While the acids in sweat inhibit the growth of bacteria, some inevitably hang around, causing body odor. The best way to prevent body odor is to keep yourself clean. Wearing natural fibers (cotton, wool, silk) will keep you drier than man-made materials, as they do a better job of absorbing and ventilating wetness. Deodorants cover up odor but do not stop sweat. Antiperspirants use the chemical aluminum chlorohydrate to actually stop sweat before it starts. There have been studies suggesting that the aluminum may soak through to your bloodstream causing harm, but the research is not conclusive.

People come up to me all the time and say, "What are those on your arm?" I have little bumps all over them.
—coyotekidd

I have keratosis pilaris. I was really self-conscious about wearing tank tops, shorts, and bathing suits. Nothing my dermatologist gave me could ever control the condition. Finally, I decided to go a different route. I went to a Chinese herbalist and acupuncturist. He told me about eating a healthier diet, drinking more water, and gave me a different kind of lotion called pearl cream. Since my first visit to him, my skin has improved drastically.
—dragonbreath5

Ever since I turned 10, I've just hated my feet because I got hereditary warts, yes, warts. I first got one on the palm of my hand, then they started to sprout up all over the heel of my right foot, and now I'm 14 and they're finally going away.
—vegantart

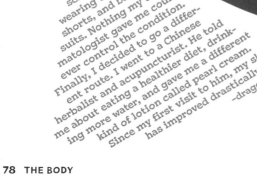

I don't think there is anything to get rid of stretch marks. They fade over time. But I hear vitamin E works, or cocoa butter is supposed to work too.
–stylystar80

HELP! I have these freakin ugly red marks surrounding my boobs! I hate them so much! I don't even know what they are! I am 14 and have a 36B. Does that have anything to do with it? Do they ever go away?
–Mewmew

I don't think size is a factor. I'm a 34A, and I have them. You get stretch marks there when your boobs grow too fast. But they will fade over time!
–Pop_rocks17

I have freckles - BIG DEAL! That's who I am and I wear them with pride...and I've even stopped trying to completely cover them with make-up - BIG accomplishment for me, seriously!
–doriangray

my right boob has a birthmark on it that looks like i spilled coffee on myself and i can't get it off. it's cool, though. i learned to live with it...i still like my left boob better, though.
–mamasita182

i used to think i had too many freckles, but now that i know many famous ppl have lots of them too, i love them.
–luvme2times

Last August, I was thrown from my horse and I gashed my right upper arm. It has a scar now, huge and pink, a long narrow armband. It gets annoying, especially when it was prominently showing in my homecoming pictures. But I've gotten used to it, loving how it makes me more original. Now it's as much a part of me as my toes or my fingernails. And it makes me look kinda tough.
–bottlegenie

SKIN MARKS

Various marks appear on the skin at different times and for different reasons. Some are temporary and others are more permanent.

Stretch Marks

Stretch marks show up when the body grows (or shrinks) faster than the skin—during growth spurts or following weight gain or loss. They can appear almost anywhere on the body, most often on boobs, hips, and bellies. Stretch marks generally begin as purplish lines and, with time, often fade to silvery lines—but they don't always fade. Some people find that rubbing vitamin E, almond oil, or cocoa butter on stretch marks helps them to fade.

Freckles

Freckles are small, brownish skin spots caused by tiny deposits of pigment. They generally darken and increase in number after sun exposure. Although they're most noticeable on fair skin, people with dark skin have freckles too.

Birthmarks

A birthmark is exactly what it sounds like—a mark on the skin that is present from birth. There are two different kinds: red and pigmented. Red birthmarks usually appear on the face, scalp, back, or chest and occur when a number of new blood vessels group together in one place. These usually disappear completely by the time a child is nine. Pigmented birthmarks, which range from brown or black to bluish gray, never disappear and can be found on any part of the body.

Moles

Moles can appear anywhere on the body. Their brown color is caused by pigment cells. Most appear before the age of 20. Sun exposure can increase the number of moles. Some moles disappear naturally. However, if there is a change in symmetry or the border, color, or size of a mole, check with a dermatologist, as this may be a sign of skin cancer.

Scars

Scars are the result of skin repairing itself after a wound. Scars generally fade over time. Some people find that vitamin E helps them to fade faster and more completely.

body hair

Every body's got body hair.

Hair normally grows almost all over the body—basically everywhere except the palms of your hands, fingertips, soles of your feet, and pink areas of your lips. Most of the hairs on the body are hard-to-see soft, light vellus hairs.

Terminal hair, the darker, more visible kind, appears on the top of the head and as eyebrows and eyelashes. With puberty, terminal hairs go on a growth spurt, appearing under the arms, in the crotch, on the legs, as well as in many cases on the upper lip, chin, arms, nipples, back, abdomen, and toes. The cause of this new growth is the hormone androgen, which is present in all girls (although to a lesser extent than in boys).

Just how much "extra" body hair you'll grow and how visible it will be has a lot to do with your heredity and ethnicity. Women of Mediterranean descent, whether Italian, Spanish, Greek, or Semitic, tend to have more dark body hair than women from Scandinavian countries. Asian women tend to have the least amount of body hair. Visible upper-lip hair, for example, is quite normal in more than a quarter of Western women, but almost impossible to find in Japan.

UNDERARM HAIR

Hair usually begins appearing under the arms after boobs start growing and pubic hair fills in. This hair, it is thought, serves a biological function, helping to spread the smell from pheromones (sex-attracting scents) given off by underarm glands. Women never bothered removing underarm hair until the 20th century, when sleeveless tops became popular and razor manufacturers advertised the clean look and smell of hairless underarms. American fashion magazines show only bare armpits, but European women seem less afraid to appear in public with hairy underarms—only about 51 percent of European women remove their underarm hair, compared with 81 percent of American women.

i got mah legs waxed a couple of years ago and here's some advice: DON'T DO IT! it hurts SOOO much even tho it stays smooth for a long time. but hey BEAUTY IS PAIN!
–minitinytantia

The hairs on my arms aren't too bad because, for one, I'm used to them by now and, secondly, they seem to go a lighter color with the sun.
–dreamin_of_you

I do shave my legs but they start to sprout again within the next day or 2 (if I'm lucky!). But I've found a solution, wax! It only hurts a tiny bit, but you don't have to remove your hair for the next 2-3 weeks!
–Canadette

i bleach my arms since my hair is so dark and my skin is so light.
–cornflakegirly

i used to shave my pubic hair but it became really itchy so i trim it sometimes. –SaraKass

i used to shave my pubic hair but it became really itchy so i trim it sometimes. stopped. now i trim it.

I feel like I am the only one with...well, you know — the mustache... I wax it about every 2 weeks.
–ghetto_gurly

LEG AND ARM HAIR

During puberty, leg hair often gets darker and thicker—and the same may be true of arm hair. Getting rid of leg hair didn't become popular until fashions changed and hemlines rose, bringing legs into view. Ads promoting leg shaving began appearing in 1915, and within 30 years more than half of U.S. women were removing leg hair. Fewer women deal with their arm hair, and if they do, they usually wax or bleach it.

I'm of Italian background, both my parents were born there. And I have thick dark hair on my arms. I don't want to wax my arms because i think everyone should have a little bit of hair on their arms - it's natural. But I still feel like it needs to be tamed!
—omniscentpower

I have black hair all around my nipples and it's scary to take my shirt off in front of people wondering what they'll think. Especially in front of my boyfriend, so I never take my shirt and bra off.
—KatieT

I have a snail trail. This upsets me as I love to wear midriff tops. I have tried various things on my sensitive belly. The worst was waxing, ouch! The slowest was using tweezers to pluck each hair. But the most effective way was using a thing called a "silky mitt" which my granny uses on her legs. You rub it in circles on the hairy area and it rubs the hair away. It is good for ultra-sensitive skin and works wonders. So I don't have a problem with my belly anymore. Good ol' gran!
—mangojam

my eyebrows r really thick. i ask my mom all the time if i can go to a specialist to get them plucked, but my mom says: "nooo they're beautiful"
—naturechild

my boobs grow hair. ch ch ch chea
—momo

My eyebrows are really bad. I pluck them and they look good...for a while. In about 3 weeks or so the hairy little suckers come back.
—surferblade

Umm...ok, well, i have advice for girls with hair above their upper lip. I use bleach. It comes with cream and powder... and u mix it and leave it on for about 20 minutes (depending on how dark it is). Basically it bleaches your hair so it blends in with the rest of you. I do it about once every 3 weeks... it works well! Make sure you wash your face after tho cuz sometimes if i don't i get a pimple by my lip.
—pinkflamingo

Well, I'm a 17-year-old girl and I have to deal with facial hair...I have hair on my upper lip, my chin, and on my cheeks...it doesn't look like a big beard, it's just dark hair. I tried using Nads, and it worked, but it hurts like hell. I've stopped using it, but my hairs have grown back finer and thinner, just like it said in the infomercial.
—petitenatalie

I recommend getting your eyebrows waxed. Once you have them waxed all you have to do is tweeze them every couple of days. And it doesn't hurt as much to tweeze hair after you get them waxed.
—n.y.c.

It is a pain to shave my bikini line, and when I do, I get red, yucky bumps. I always opt for boy-bottom swimming suits so I don't have to shave!
—loudbb

I was shaving down there, becuz of a thong that was really little that showed a lot, so i did it for a guy, and i was soo itchy after, that i couldn't even do anything "in bed" with him! NEVER DO IT!
—Saggitaurus

PUBIC HAIR

The first signs of pubic hair usually appear before menstruation begins, when the breasts are just beginning to grow. Initially, this hair tends to be fine and straight, but within a few years it gets darker and coarser and begins to spread as far as the inner thighs and lower abdomen.

FOR MORE ON PUBIC HAIR, SEE THE CROTCH ON PAGES 68–69

HAIR IN OTHER PLACES

Hair growth in other places can feel more embarrassing because not everyone gets it and it is less talked about. But a lot of women, especially those of Mediterranean or Middle Eastern descent, have darker, thicker hair on their face (eyebrows, upper lip, sideburns, chin), neck, and around the nipples.

I have hair, fingers, on my arms, "down upper lip, legs, "down there," armpits, and a slight "snail trail" on my stomach. Lucky me, tho, it's all blond and really, really fine so it's pretty hard to see. I just use a razor on my under-arms, legs, & "down there" once in a while, and I'm never gonna shave my stomach 'cause I've heard horror stories...
—madconnectionz

Don't freak out and be depressed about your hair—light, dark, lots of hair, lil bit of hair. DON'T worry!!! There are ways to remove it and by chance people won't notice it! One time when I was younger I went to the pool with some friends in a regular biki-ni and when I changed, I noticed I had brown hairs on my stomach and back and I freaked. I called my friend in, who is VERY honest, and I said, "Look at my stomach and back. Do you notice any-thing?" and she looked for a sec then gave me a weird glare and said, "Hun, what are you talking about?" I smiled and I had a good time swimming.
—Lil_cozy_gurl

The hair on my body grows so frickin fast! I shave my legs and pits in the morning and by the time I take my shower after track it's all back! Grrrrr! I feel like an overgrown MONKEY!
—crazywonderer

I would love to remove my hair from my legs and under my arms but I have this problem called my mother!
—ghetto_gurly

yea i'm hairy!! but who isn't?? i shave the legs and the armpits, bleach the upper lip, and pluck the brows....ahhh the pubes. that's a story for another day
—pinkcarrotte

My hair grows on my armpits, vagina, head, legs, arms, and my nipples. I remove the hair on my legs with wax. I like the other hairs the way they are.
—destinee

i usually just let it all grow unless i have to wear a skirt or swimsuit. i shave my armpits every day though.
—LaDaRu

my hair grows everywhere, and it comes back after i shave it. i am very hairy, and sometimes i let it stay there until i feel like shav-ing it.
—helovesme

I have lots of hair. I have a swirl down my back (actually quite sexy cause I have a nice back), really dark black very curly pubic hair (trim it), dark hair on my arms (leave it), legs (shave it), bushy eyebrows (which I tame daily), and really long dark eyelashes (def leave them!). Some people think it's real-ly sexy, but others are like - urr you have a mustache!
—rock_n_talk

BODY HAIR IN ART

Most nude images of women minimize pubic hair. Throughout history, painters have depicted nudes with at most a tiny, neat triangle in this area, and nude photo-graphs in magazines are usually carefully retouched to minimize any hair. In contrast, artist Frida Kahlo carefully painted in her distinctive eye-brows and her upper-lip hair as integral to her self-portraits.

TOO MUCH HAIR

Most hair growth at adolescence is nor-mal, but occasionally there can be a hor-monal disorder that causes a lot of dark, coarse hair to appear on the face (especial-ly the upper lip and chin), as well as on the arms, chests, back, abdomen, and thighs. This condition, called hirsutism, is usually caused by the body's producing too much androgen and can be helped by prescription drugs that control androgen levels. Some med-ications that contain hormones, such as birth control pills or anabolic steroids, may also increase hair growth.

HAIR REMOVAL

Women have been trying to get rid of body hair for a long time, perhaps in an attempt to accentuate the female/male difference. Ancient Egyptian women applied and then stripped off a concoction containing bird bones, oil, cucumber, and other ingredients to remove unwanted body hair. Ancient Roman women used hot tar and super-sharp shells.

The choice to remove body hair is a personal one; it all depends on whether you feel comfortable with what you have. As far as health and hygiene go, there's no reason that you need to get rid of body hair, and the process of removal can be a real pain. It may hurt or give rise to ingrown hairs, dry skin, or rashes, cuts, and infections.

TWEEZING OR PLUCKING

WHAT IT IS: Pulling hairs out one by one with tweezers.

FREQUENCY: As needed. Once you tweeze a hair, it won't grow back for a month or more, but other hairs may appear nearby.

COST: If you do it yourself, nothing, once you've bought the tweezers.

PAIN: Hurts for a second or two, especially in sensitive areas like around the nipples.

TIPS: Cleaning your tweezers with rubbing alcohol before and after use helps avoid infections.

TRIMMING

WHAT IT IS: Using scissors to cut unwanted hair, such as pubic hair that hangs out of your bathing suit.

FREQUENCY: As needed.

COST: Nothing, after you buy the scissors.

PAIN: None.

DEPILATORY

WHAT IT IS: A cream, liquid, or gel that you put on the area where you want to remove hair. It uses chemicals to break up the bonds that hold the hair shaft together, so that it literally falls apart. You can then wash or wipe hair and depilatory away.

FREQUENCY: Lasts a week or two.

COST: Not prohibitive. A variety of inexpensive brands can be found in drugstores.

PAIN: Stinging may occur if your skin is sensitive to the chemicals. Be sure you follow the directions, using it only on recommended areas and for the specified amount of time.

TIPS: Do a patch test, first trying out a new product on a small area to see if there are any bad skin reactions. And, again, follow the directions carefully.

SHAVING

WHAT IT IS: Using a razor to cut off hair right at the skin.

FREQUENCY: Daily to weekly, depending on how fast the hair grows. (Can be done less often in winter, when hair grows more slowly, and in cold climates.)

COST: Just the cost of razors and cream or soap—or of an electric shaver.

PAIN: None, if you don't cut yourself. But can cause some irritation.

TIPS: For handheld razors, it's best to shave just after (or while) opening up the pores of your skin under warm water. With electric shavers, though, you need to make sure your skin is absolutely dry.

BLEACHING

WHAT IT IS: Chemically lightening the color of hair. Usually used only for facial hair.

FREQUENCY: Depends on how fast your hair grows. May last a month. Repeat when hair becomes two-tone.

COST: Slightly more than depilatories. Buy a name brand.

PAIN: Can cause irritation in sensitive areas and a slight burning sensation on application.

TIPS: As with a depilatory, test the product in a small area first to make sure there's no allergic reaction. Follow the directions carefully, and don't leave the bleach on too long.

WAXING

WHAT IT IS: Spreading wax (usually heated) over the area where you want hair removed and then, once it's dry, using a cloth strip to pull it off—along with hair and roots. Bikini waxes have become particularly popular as bathing suits get more revealing.

FREQUENCY: Lasts 3 to 8 weeks.

COST: You can buy an at-home kit for about the same amount you might spend on depilatories, or you can go to a professional, which may cost you as much as a haircut at a beauty salon.

PAIN: It's like ripping an adhesive bandage off a large area of skin (ouch). Some redness and skin irritation may result.

TIPS: If you use a home kit, work on small areas at a time. Avoid waxing when you're sunburned or if you're taking acne medication, as your skin may be ultra-sensitive.

ELECTROLYSIS

WHAT IT IS: It's when a qualified practitioner inserts a filament, or long thin needle, into an individual hair follicle, reaching for the base, and zaps it with an electric current. (Alternatively, heat can be used, in which case it's called thermolysis.) If the job is done right, then that particular hair is gone forever—but hitting just the right spot is tricky, even for a skilled practitioner, and there are hundreds of hair follicle sites even in a small area. It's used mostly for facial hair, but also for bikini lines.

FREQUENCY: To remove, say, a mustache usually requires weekly visits for a few months (because hair keeps growing and, even for treated hair follicles, there's a 40 percent regrowth rate). Figure 4 to 10 hours (sessions are usually only 15 to 30 minutes), plus later touch-up visits. For a bikini line, double the time.

COST: Expensive. Probably several hundred dollars for a mustache, less if you're having a few stray whiskers removed.

PAIN: It definitely hurts, but how much depends on how pain-sensitive you are. Most people can't tolerate more than 15 to 30 minutes at a time. Taking ibuprofen or a similar pain reliever a half-hour before may lessen the pain. There are also creams like EMLA that you can rub on your skin to temporarily numb an area.

TIPS: Make sure you go to a board-certified electrologist. A top electrologist may charge more per hour, but may actually save you money by zapping more hairs, with a lower regrowth rate, and avoiding scars.

LASER HAIR REMOVAL

WHAT IT IS: Essentially this technique involves zapping the hair follicle with an intense beam of light, or laser. About a dozen different laser techniques have been approved by the Food and Drug Administration, but several are good only for people with light skin. It works best on dark (heavily pigmented) hair, which absorbs the most light.

FREQUENCY: Lasts about 6 months or more.

COST: Super-expensive. Usually several hundred dollars per treatment, with multiple sessions bringing the total over a thousand dollars.

PAIN: Varies, depending on the particular technique, but less painful than electrolysis.

TIPS: Check your practitioner's credentials.

SOME ALTERNATIVE HAIR-REMOVING TECHNIQUES

SUGARING: Commonly used in North Africa and the Middle East, this technique resembles waxing. A mixture of sugar and honey is spread on the skin and covered with cotton strips, which are then pulled off along with the hair. It hurts, but not as much as waxing.

THREADING: Used by women in the Middle East, India, China, and other places, this method pulls off hairs using a coiled thread. Best for facial hair, it's less likely to irritate the skin than wax or even tweezers, quickly picks up even tiny hairs, and can be precisely controlled for a clean line. It does sometimes hurt, but not for long.

decorating the body

It's a human urge to decorate our bodies, and we've been doing it for over 40,000 years. The reasons people do this vary by culture, and include:
- to attract a mate
- to make the body beautiful (sometimes making art in the process)
- to symbolize cultural identity, wealth, superior ability, or some other kind of social status
- to mark a "rite of passage," including adolescence, marriage, and death
- to protect the wearer (against evil spirits, pests, et cetera)

Much of this decoration has been temporary, like hair coloring, makeup, and adornments, while some of it is more permanent, like tattoos and scarification (and some pierced jewelry).

FOR INFO ON HAND AND NAIL DECORATION, SEE PAGE 65

TEMPORARY DECORATION

From head to toe, from ancient times to this minute, women have found creative ways to enhance their appearance.

hair color

Among U.S. women today, more than half—and as many as three-fourths—color their hair, mostly to beautify themselves and often to make style statements. There are a huge number of hair shades to choose from, with 500 versions of blond alone, and a number of different hair color options. Hair color can last anywhere from one shampoo to when your hair grows out, Here are the longer-lasting options:

PERMANENT COLOR uses dye containing both ammonia and peroxide to give color that penetrates into the hair shaft and lasts until your hair grows out. If the color is noticeably different than your natural color, you may want touch-ups every six weeks or so, though some people like the roots look.

BLEACHING is the process of using peroxide to get rid of pigment in hair so it looks blond. Sometimes people apply a toner after bleach to tone down the yellowish effect. This is called double-process.

HENNA is a natural hair dye, made from plant leaves. In its neutral (uncolored) form, it's used as a conditioner. In red or black forms it can darken or brighten (but not lighten) hair color, staining the outside of the hair shaft. It has no hair-damaging chemicals, but the results are permanent and not always predictable.

Highlighting lightens certain strands of hair (rather than all your hair) to add depth to the hair, or to give a chunking or striping effect.

Long-term use of permanent hair color can be harmful to your hair, and possibly other parts of your body. Ammonia, used in hair dye (as well as cleaning products), and peroxide, a kind of bleach, are both damaging to hair. Some studies have shown a link between dark-colored permanent hair dye and certain kinds of cancer.

FOR MORE ON HAIR AND HAIRSTYLES, SEE PAGES 48-51

HAIR COLOR AROUND THE WORLD

For important events, Egyptian women around 3000 BC wore wigs with elaborate braids that were sometimes dyed blue, green, or blond. Ancient Greeks used to lighten their hair with saffron. In ancient Rome, when fair-haired people were captured from northern Europe and Britain, blond hair became very popular. Roman women used gold dust to give their hair the illusion of blondness or bleached it. They also cut off the hair of their Teutonic servants and had it made into wigs. When dark hair became fashionable again, wealthy Roman women used walnut-colored dye on themselves and prostitutes were required to have blond hair in contrast. During the Renaissance, women used natural dyes to lighten their hair. French women in the 1780s wore elaborate hairstyles powdered with blue, purple, pink, and other pastel shades. In the late 1860s a theater group from England known as the British Blondes sparked a peroxiding craze in the United States. Synthetic hair dye was invented in 1907.

makeup

Makeup is color applied to the face and at times other parts of the body. It can sometimes be about creating illusion—for example, making the eyes appear closer together or farther apart. One of its main effects is to duplicate a look of sexual arousal: wide eyes, flushed skin, swollen red lips. From the beginning of the 20th century, makeup has been a crucial part of creating our culture's images of beauty in magazines, movies, TV shows, music videos, and advertising. The first beauty "makeover" feature was introduced by **Mademoiselle** in 1936. By the late 1940s, many women were wearing makeup everyday. The rise of youth culture starting in the 1950s created a specific teen makeup market, which continues today.

Wearing makeup, especially at work, can be profitable. A New York Times article in 2000 revealed that women who wore makeup earned 30 percent more than those who didn't.

Makeup styles go in and out of fashion, influenced by celebrity images of beauty and oftentimes dictated by the fashion and beauty industries, which create continual demand for new beauty products.

EYE MAKEUP AROUND THE WORLD

Egyptians put on eye makeup not just for decoration but also for health reasons—to protect their eyes from the glare of the sun, to keep flies away, and to counter eye ailments. Women painted their upper eyelids and eyebrows black (first with galena and then with kohl) and their lower lids green with malachite. Queen Nefertiti made up her eyes this way at her wedding to King Amenhotep in 1372 BC. This style became a huge influence on Western culture in the early 20th century when the Ballets Russes, an avant-garde Russian dance group, performed in the U.S. and France, sparking an interest in wearing kohl around the eyes (along with more colorful makeup in general). Hollywood stars like Theda Bara and Josephine Baker famously worked this look.

LIP MAKEUP

LIPSTICK adds color and sometimes moisture to the lips, and can make them appear fuller or slimmer. Women have reddened their lips for thousands of years with natural materials, most notably red ochre. In 1915 lipstick became available for the first time in small metal containers. By midcentury it was the most popular makeup product in the U.S., worn by 80 to 90 percent of women. In 1952 Revlon began introducing new colors every season, starting the trend of constantly changing lipstick fashion. Lipsticks are available in many formulas, from sheer to matte to cream to shimmer and more. Some lipsticks include moisturizing and sun protection agents.

LIP GLOSS adds shine to the lips or on top of lipstick.

LIP LINER adds definition to the shape of the lips. It can be used to reshape the mouth.

EYE MAKEUP

EYELINER outlines the eyes to make them stand out and look bigger. It comes in pencil, liquid, felt-tip, powder, or cake form.

EYEBROW PENCILS are used to fill in brows. Eyebrow makeup can also come in cake form and is used to add definition to the brows. Some people go for a dramatic look by removing or covering over their natural brows and brushing on new ones in their place.

EYE SHADOW adds color around the eyes to intensify or highlight the iris color, suggest a mood, or "reshape" the eyes (usually with the help of eyeliner). Eye shadow is available in powder, cream, or pencil forms. It can be applied with a brush, sponge-tip applicator, pencil tip, or your fingers. There are hundreds of shadowing options, from natural skin tones to smoky dark shades to brilliant bright colors.

MASCARA colors eyelashes and makes them look longer and thicker. It can also be used to color and style brows. T. L. Williams started the Maybelline mascara company in 1914 after seeing his sister Mabel put petroleum jelly on her eyelashes to make them stand out. Mascara comes in lots of colors. Waterproof brands can be hard to remove.

FALSE EYELASHES make eyelashes appear longer and thicker.

EYELASH CURLERS crunch upper lashes into a curl.

TWEEZERS OR WAX are used to remove eyebrow hairs or to give them a specific shape.

SKIN MAKEUP

BLUSH adds color to the cheeks, or anywhere else it's applied, and most often comes in shades of pink, brown, and red. It is available in powder, liquid, and cream.

FOUNDATION gives skin a smooth, more even look. Pressed powders became available in compact form in 1914. Foundation is now available in powder, liquid, and cream, and in a huge range of skin tones. Some include moisturizing or acne-treating agents. Throughout history, women have used a remarkable variety of moisturizing products to make their skin smoother and more youthful looking.

GLITTER can be brushed or rubbed anywhere on the body for a subtle or dramatic sparkle.

SELF-TANNER gives skin a suntanned look without the harmful rays. Self-tanners are sometimes difficult to use—getting a natural look (without red hands) can be challenging, but the products are improving.

FOR MORE ON SKIN CARE, SEE PAGE 77

ANIMAL TESTING

Some cosmetic companies test products on animals to determine if they're safe for humans before bringing them to market. Because animals can be harmed in the process, animal rights supporters protest and boycott those companies that do animal testing. There are also many "cruelty-free" cosmetic manufacturers—who call attention to this fact on their labels.

SKIN MAKEUP
AROUND THE WORLD

FOR MORE ON NECKLACES, SEE PAGE 58, AND FOR MORE ON BRACELETS AND RINGS, SEE PAGE 65

Red ochre is the oldest makeup on record, presumably used by prehistoric people in southern Africa to paint the skin. Queen Nefertiti used yellow ochre to give herself a golden glow and applied red ochre to her cheeks on the occasion of her wedding.

Babylonians lightened their skin with white lead or darkened it with hematite and red ochre. Palestinian women in the 2nd century achieved a pinkish skin tone by mixing white lead and red pigment with starch. Japanese women developed many methods over time for whitening skin. In the 3rd century they applied nightingale droppings; in the 9th century they used a chalky rice-flour powder called **oshiroi** to whiten their skin and a safflower-based rouge called **beni**; and in the late 12th century they painted their faces with a sake and green tea mixture. Upper-class European women were dedicated whiteners as well. In the 1300s leeches were a popular skin-lightening treatment. During the 1600s they applied a white lead-based mixture which proved to be poisonous. Dark-skinned women in the Caribbean, Kenya, and elsewhere in Africa use lightening creams, many of which are poisonous as well.

FOR MORE ON POISONOUS MAKEUP, SEE PAGE 25

BARE FACES

Not everybody wears makeup. Many women choose not to because they prefer how their faces look without it or they can't be bothered with the process.

Makeup for women has not always been commonly accepted. Most notably, Christianity in the Middle Ages condemned cosmetics while promoting modesty, putting the official kibosh on makeup use in Europe until the Renaissance. In the late 1700s American Revolutionary women rejected all cosmetics as symbols of the anti-democratic upper class, and French revolutionaries shunned it as a sign of aristocratic excess. Actresses in the theater and ladies of the night continued to experiment with more colorful makeup and were regarded by the Church as too openly sexual and by the upper classes as very unrespectable. Things continued in this vein until the turn of the 20th century. The growth of a youth makeup market in the 1950s brought objections from people who felt it was inappropriate for teenagers to wear makeup. Many parents today hold the same view.

adornment

Women (and men) have been adorning their bodies for thousands of years. Egyptian women sometimes wove stones or jewelry or gold thread through their braided wigs. Traditionally, Indian women wore bindhis on their foreheads along with nose rings when they got married.

Some traditional cultures have used jewelry as a way of shaping the body. For instance, the Dayak in Borneo wear heavy earrings to elongate the ears.

PIERCING

Figurines with multiple ear piercings and nose studs from 4,000 to 4,500 years ago have been found in the Near East. Nose piercing was also popular in ancient Mexico and India. Today, many women in India and Pakistan still adorn themselves with nose rings—sometimes as a sign that they are married, sometimes as a show of wealth, sometimes just for decoration. Lip piercing—but not tongue piercing—was once common among Eskimo women and men in Alaska. Acquiring a labret (lip plug) was part of the initiation rite of puberty. Sometimes the labrets had extra holes, to which a string of beads could be attached; the women might also have beaded strings dangling from their noses. Among the Tlingit on the Northwest Coast, women's Labrets not only marked the passage into womanhood, but carried a variety of other meanings. Some groups believed they helped keep women from talking too much; others saw them as a sign of power.

Piercing stepped into the limelight in our modern culture. In the late 1970s punks appeared with safety pins piercing not only their ears but other body parts, like the eyebrow or lips. As a rebellion against conventional tastes and values, the look was shocking to many at the time. By the 1990s the piercing craze had spread to mainstream pop culture.

CAUTION:

With piercing and tattooing, the most serious risk comes from equipment that isn't sterile, which can lead to infections—including such serious ones as hepatitis and AIDS. Skin allergies are also a possibility, either from tattoo pigments or from metal in jewelry. Other not-so-pleasant side effects from piercing can be nerve damage, permanent holes, chipped teeth (from tongue studs), choking (from wayward mouth jewels), thick scars, and damage to milk-producing glands (with nipple rings).

PERMANENT DECORATION
TATTOOING

Tattooing has been around for at least 5,000 years, mainly among pale-skinned peoples because tattoos do not generally show up on darker skin. The tattooing process consists of piercing the skin with a needle and then injecting colored dye into the wound. When the wound heals, the design is seen through the skin. It is a painful and time-consuming procedure.

In non-Western cultures, tattoos are often important symbols of cultural identity and rites of passage. The word "tattoo," which comes from the Tahitian word **tatau**, came into use during the 18th century, when Captain James Cook wrote about the markings he saw among the different peoples in Polynesia. Especially noteworthy were the tattoos all over the face, called **moko**, among Maori men in New Zealand. These tattoos were a mark not only of status but also of the person's individuality, as each was different. Maori women tattooed only their lips and chin—without these marks, they believed their faces would be naked and ugly. Simple patterns were usually used to mark the transition to adulthood, and other marks were added at special events, such as marriage and childbirth.

In traditional cultures, girls are often tattooed to mark the transition into womanhood and for spiritual reasons. Women without those tattoos may be seen as ugly. For Berber women in North Africa, tattooed dots on the chin, nose, and cheeks (near the eyes) are not only considered attractive, but they are thought to prevent evil spirits from entering the body. Kutch women in India see their tattoos as both a sign of wealth and as a mark of personal beauty. They only tattoo parts of the body that will be visible in public. In Fiji, if a woman did not have a tattoo, she risked being beaten up and served as food to the gods after her death.

In Japan during the 18th century, tattoos were often used to pledge love or allegiance to someone. For people in lower classes, who were not allowed to wear elaborate kimonos, colorful tattoo pictures all over the body became a way of permanently clothing the body in fancy "dress." Although it was mostly men who wore these tattoos, geishas might have had their backs painted.

People get tattoos in our culture for many reasons: it can be a sign of affiliation, an act of rebellion, or a celebration of an important event. In London in 1901 some upper-class women, like Lady Randolph Churchill, got tattoos to commemorate the coronation of King Edward VII. Some people see tattooing as a way of getting in touch with a primitive spirituality, and some people just like the decorations.

Tattooists in many U.S. states and parts of Canada are not allowed by law to work on anyone under 18 years of age. To avoid legal hassles, many body piercers insist that clients be 18 or older, or that they present written permission from their parents. Tattoos are permanent; however, laser procedures can remove most of the image, though it may leave some scarring.

scarification

Scarification is the process of cutting the skin and creating raised scars, often in elaborate patterns. Keloid scars have an exaggerated raised effect, created through making several cuts or inserting a small pebble under the cut. Scarification occurs mainly in Africa, where tattoos are not noticeable against dark skin, but intentionally raised scars show up nicely. These patterned scars have important cultural meanings and are often used to mark milestones in a person's life.

Among the Hemba people in Zaire and Zambia in Central Africa, there is a traditional saying that women are not born with physical beauty—they only acquire it through **bindala** signs (the scars adorning their bodies). The scars are seen as a mark of courage, evidence of a woman's ability to withstand life's pains. A lot of sexual pleasure is said to be attached to touching these raised markings.

In some places scarification is part of a complex coming-of-age ritual for girls. When their breasts begin to bud, Nuba girls in the southern Sudan receive their first markings, a series of dots pointing from the navel to the breasts. Once they begin menstruating, they gain rows of markings below the breast. These scars signal sexual maturation and make the young woman more appealing to potential mates. After giving birth to their first child, Nuba women get ornamental scars in geometric patterns on the back, arms, legs, and neck.

For the Tiv in Nigeria, the scars are also beauty marks and a way of making women more appealing. During puberty, girls are decorated with what's called a "catfish" design on their bellies to increase their attractiveness and fertility. Among the Yoruba, also in Nigeria, women traditionally decorate their bodies with elaborate scar designs, creating artworks on their skin that appeal to both the eyes and the sense of touch. Often the designs include animals, like doves, snakes, or butterflies, but there may also be symbols representing gods or everyday objects like scissors or wristwatches. Some women have scar designs over most of their bodies, including markings on the face. Scarring is painful; **O ni laiya dada** ("she is very courageous") is a high form of praise regarding a Yoruba woman's looks.

body modification

People throughout history have individually wanted to change their bodies to get closer to the beauty ideals of their time and place. Documents from India some 2,600 years ago speak of creating a nose from the skin on the cheeks, and Renaissance doctors did "beauty surgery" to fix up noses damaged from syphilis or street fights.

COSMETIC SURGERY

As the phrase "cosmetic surgery" underlines, these changes are done for the sake of appearance. But getting a nose fixed (or any other body part) was a major ordeal until the invention of anesthesia lessened the pain and antiseptics reduced the risk of infection.

Actually, the demand for cosmetic surgery didn't really take hold until after World War I, when the cosmetic business as a whole took off.

In 1923 comedienne Fanny Brice had a nose job that got a lot of publicity. Brice said she did it for her career, but some people thought she did it to look less Jewish. As Dorothy Parker put it, she "cut off her nose to spite her race." Today, people voice similar concerns about cosmetic surgery as a way of fitting people into the dominant beauty ideal rather than appreciating the differences that make each person unique.

Cosmetic surgery as a beauty tool caught on quickly. In 1924 the **New York Daily Mirror** sponsored a "Homely Girl" contest, for which the prize was a surgical makeover. In the 1930s cosmetic surgery was increasingly used to create the glamourous Hollywood star. By 1940 magazines like **Good Housekeeping** were asking (in an article on nose jobs), "Why should anyone suffer under the handicap of a conspicuously ugly feature?" It wasn't until the late 1970s that a few accounts of botched operations and unpleasant side effects of cosmetic tinkering began appearing in the media—risks that continue to be downplayed.

The 1980s, with its emphasis on the body (particularly the gym-shaped ideal), ushered in an increased demand for cosmetic surgery that continues today. In the 1990s alone, the number of surgeries increased by more than 150 percent.

At the beginning of the 21st century, there are an unprecedented number of cosmetic surgery procedures, with new ones being invented as we write. The most popular ones in the U.S. are liposuction, eyelid surgery, breast implants, and nose jobs. Only women of some wealth can afford cosmetic surgery, as most procedures cost at least $2,000.

LIPOSUCTION is a procedure in which a cosmetic surgeon vacuums out a pocket of fat through an incision in the skin. Aftereffects include swelling, bruising, and possible numbness for a few days, and may last longer depending on how much fat was removed.

EYELID SURGERY removes bagginess and tightens loose skin around the eyelid by reshaping it. Aftereffects include blurry vision and teary or dry eyes for a few days and bruising and swelling that may last a week or two.

BREAST IMPLANT SURGERY involves inserting saline-filled bags in between the breast tissue and the chest muscles, or between the chest muscles and the chest wall. A similar procedure, reconstructive breast surgery, is sometimes done after a mastectomy. Aftereffects include body and breast soreness for a few days to a week or two.

BREAST REDUCTION SURGERY, technically known as reduction mammaplasty, is a procedure in which fat, glandular tissue, and skin are removed from the breasts, making them smaller. Recovery can take about nine weeks.

FACELIFTS tighten and smooth the skin by stretching it up toward the scalp and back behind the ears. Aftereffects include bruising for about two weeks; swelling, which can last longer; and possible numbness, which may last several weeks.

INJECTIONS of fat (usually taken from the patient's butt) and collagen fill wrinkles and add fullness to the lips and face. Botox injections smooth frown lines and wrinkles around the eyes by paralyzing the muscles in the forehead. Possible aftereffects include mild swelling, bruising, and numbness. These costly injections are not permanent and must be repeated every three to four months to maintain results.

FOR INFORMATION ON NOSE JOBS, SEE PAGE 54

CAUTION: With any permanent body change it's important to think seriously about your reasons for doing it, and to remember that what looks good to you now might not always look good to you. Some body transformations can be at least partially undone (implants can be removed; tattoos can be "erased" through a painful process), but other procedures can't be reversed. Many permanent changes also carry health risks. Surgery is really about cutting and wounding the body, and a slipup can damage nerves, leaving an area numb. In a few cases (but enough to worry about) women have died under the beautifying knife.

STRETCHING

In contrast to older generations of Chinese women who bound their feet to appear more petite, 21st-century Chinese believe that bigger is better. Recently, Chinese bone extension surgery has become popular as more Chinese are equating height with social stature. The surgery, which is quite painful and carries many risks, involves severing the shin and inserting a mechanism that gradually pushes apart the two sides of the bone as it regenerates, filling the space. Over the course of six to eight months, the bone can be extended up to four inches. For this entire period, the patient must remain in bed, in braces. Afterward, there is a rehabilitation period of up to several months. Complications include extremely brittle bones or bones that don't grow straight. Also, the surgery is quite expensive, though those who undertake the procedure believe it is a worthwhile investment of time and money.

BODY SHAPING
AROUND THE WORLD

Throughout history and around the world, people have changed virtually every part of the body to pursue the beauty ideals of their particular culture.

In ancient Egypt, a longer head was thought to be more beautiful and girls' heads were artificially elongated. In later periods, girls' ears were bound flat against their heads to make them less noticeable. Hundreds of years ago, face-flattening, done during the first few weeks of life, when the skull was still soft, was performed to beautify infants in Europe, the Americas, and Africa. People from different cultures have also shaped hairlines, made necks longer, widened noses, worn lip plugs, chipped teeth, constricted bellies, lengthened labia lips, narrowed waists, lengthened legs, swelled thighs, and bound feet.

In some ancient and non-Western cultures, body alterations often have symbolic meaning that has to do with rites of passage and cultural identity, as well as being a way of beautifying the body. They can also have spiritual significance.

Lobi and Kirdi women from West Africa, for instance, acquired lip plugs to block evil forces from coming in through the mouth. Lip plugs of certain tribes in Africa and the Americas were seen as marks of cultural identity that emphasized the naturally bigger, fuller lips of these tribes in comparison to their thinner-lipped neighbors'. When the African slave trade grew in the 16th century, people didn't want to buy slaves with lip plugs—a factor that may have increased their popularity among other tribes. In some of these tribes, beauty is also linked to the size of the lip plug.

Similarly, foot binding is thought to have important cultural origins arising from the natural difference between Chinese women's small feet and the larger feet of the neighboring Tartar women. The Chinese likely began binding the feet of girls at a young age to exaggerate this natural smallness—and it had the added effect of keeping many women close to home, since it wasn't easy to walk far with bound feet. Meanwhile, Tartar women wore extra-long shoes to draw attention to their characteristically long feet. Footbinding was practiced most extensively by families wealthy enough to not have their women work, and it was officially outlawed by the government in 1911.

CHECK THE VARIOUS BODY PARTS ON PAGES 46-77 FOR MORE INFO ON HOW THEY'VE BEEN CHANGED AROUND THE WORLD

SEE PAGE 25 FOR MORE ON HOW EXTREME FASHIONS HAVE CHANGED THE BODY

CREATING

A LOOK

WHAT IS STYLE?

Fashion may be about trends, but style is about personal expression. Your personal style is your opportunity to express yourself to the world. It's also an opportunity to play with the wide range of tools and possibilities for transformation. When you work with style, it's no longer a matter of raw materials, or what you were born with. Style is about creating, not about accepting things the way they are.

Diana Vreeland, 20th-century guru of style said, "Never worry about the facts, just project an image to the public." Your style is your image. It's how you want the world to see you, what you feel comfortable with, who you feel like you might be on any given day.

One of the great things about style is that it can change—evolving slowly over time, or jumping around from one look to another according to your whims. And if you find one style that is totally you, stick with it as long as you feel good about it. Style doesn't have to change, it's just nice to know that it can.

FINDING YOUR STYLE

Finding your own style can be a lifetime project (but a fun one). In figuring out who you are, you get a chance to play with different ideas of yourself. Dressing up is one of the earliest ways children play with their identities. It's a similar process when adults play with their looks.

There are so many possibilities in the world of style: Influences and ideas can be found in history, art, media, and even in nature. Fashion magazines are an obvious source, but it's important to remember that they're showing what's "in style," which can have more to do with trends in the fashion industry than with style as expression. So while one style might be more "fashionable," there are tons of other looks out there that are just as fabulous—and timeless (rather than trendy).

Style has meaning, and that's part of its power. Do you think the same things about a girl in an evening gown as you do about a girl in overalls? Or a miniskirt? Most likely, you have ideas about who a person might be

based on what she's wearing. That's the power of style. By changing what you wear, you can change people's impression of you.

At the same time, changing your style or trying out something new does not change who you are inside. Some styles are viewed as a sign that you identify with a certain label or group, such as preps, goths, skaters, or hippies, for example. This may be what you want—or it may be frustrating to you because you know that your style is not the sum total of who you are. While some people may react as if your style defines you, you are not what you wear!

To help you think about the many kinds of beauty and style out there in the universe, we put together a collection of different looks that have made an impact on the world of style. These looks are not by any means comprehensive, and they aren't necessarily the "ultimate" examples of beauty. But they're a variety of looks for you to think about, play with, try on, and combine as you see fit.

GETTING THE LOOKS

These looks are intended as a kind of flexible recipe book of different style sensibilities. We tried to represent a variety of styles on a variety of different kinds of girls. While some looks are associated with physical characteristics (such as a certain hairstyle or body type), they can also be adapted for any girl. Many of the fashions can be found inexpensively at vintage or thrift shops, with patience. The how-to section on the right-hand page will show you how to make each look your own. We consulted with experts in hair, makeup, and styling to describe the techniques and traits that define each iconic look.

Use this part of the book as a resource, but don't feel tied to the way a look is represented here. Some of the most stylish people are those who creatively combine different looks, who pick up on pieces of a particular style, or who reject the idea of "style icons" altogether and invent their own looks.

FOR MORE IDEAS ABOUT MAKING THESE LOOKS WORK FOR YOU, SEE FREEDOM OF STYLE, PAGE 146.

TAKING RESPONSIBILITY FOR YOUR STYLE

An important factor in figuring out your style is the reaction of people around you. You may not care about this at all, or you may be really concerned about it. Your family and friends, as well as people at school or work, will probably all have opinions about your style and how you "should" dress. These attitudes may be expressed formally, as in a uniform or dress code. Or they may be less specific, and you might not know what's considered OK to wear until you cross a line you didn't know was there. Either way, you need to think about who you're dealing with, what their attitude might be, and how important it is to respect their opinions before taking any radical style steps.

Part of taking on your own style is taking responsibility for it. Style makes an impact, on people who are close to you and on the world at large. The relationship of style to sexuality raises some particular concerns. If you choose to present yourself in a sexually explicit way, you can expect to get attention whether or not you want it. While the responsibility for any unwanted sexual advances is always on the perpetrator, it is smart to think about the way people might respond to the way you are dressing. Other types of attention-getting looks can also provoke comments and negative responses. If you choose to take your style to extremes or take on a look with strong connotations, it is important to consider how your decisions will be read by the people around you.

bombshell

The Bombshell was born in Hollywood, but she got her name in the Pacific Islands. During World War II, posters of Hollywood actresses were sent to troops overseas to help boost morale. Even at home, people needed distraction from the war. Hollywood was happy to oblige with musical extravaganzas and pin-up posters of their glamorous stars. After her explosive success in **Gilda**, **Rita Hayworth** became the first literal bombshell when one of her pin-ups was pasted to the first atom bomb tested on Bikini atoll in 1946. Soon after, Rita introduced the bikini bathing suit, named after the site of her bombshell fame. Rita's fiery red waves and va-va-voom body made her the ultra Bombshell for the wartime 40s.

The 1950s called for a different kind of Bombshell—one that acknowledged the country's postwar return to conservative values and traditional homes and families. **Marilyn Monroe** was the ultimate Blonde Bombshell, all softness and femininity, breathiness and boobs. Her cozy glamour made her the Bombshell-next-door: unbelievably gorgeous yet almost accessible in her all-American sexpot way. Her unique combination of high-gloss beauty and vulnerability makes her the enduring queen of the Bombshell genre.

marilyn monroe in the seven-year itch

BOMBSHELL
IN ACTION

Rita Hayworth in **Gilda** (1946)

Marilyn Monroe in **Gentlemen Prefer Blondes** (1953)

Brigitte Bardot in . . . **And God Created Woman** (1956)

Jayne Mansfield in **The Girl Can't Help It** (1956)

Sophia Loren in **Two Women** (1961)

Rita Moreno in **The Vagabond King** (1956)

Raquel Welch in **Mother, Jugs and Speed** (1976)

Model **Tyra Banks**

This Bombshell formula has been emulated and reinterpreted over time. From 1950s copycats like **Jayne Mansfield** to modern revisions, the Bombshell is an archetype that speaks volumes in an instant. The Bombshell look is a seductive combination of power and weakness—while a Bombshell has the ability to bowl men over, she can also seem somehow dependent, as if she needs a man's attention to activate her power.

Madonna's 1980s Bombshell revamp co-opted Marilyn's **Gentlemen Prefer Blondes** look and turned it on its ear. Because of Madonna's obvious ability to manipulate her own image and career, she was able to give the Bombshell a new self-sufficient twist.

HAIR IS ALWAYS SEXY AND GLAMOROUS. COLOR TENDS TO BE EXTREME: PLATINUM BLOND, FIRE-ENGINE RED, OR RAVEN BLACK.

EXPOSED SHOULDERS

FEMININE TRAITS ARE PROMINENTLY DISPLAYED.

LONG EYELASHES (FALSE OR MASCARA), LIQUID EYELINER FOR A CLASSIC CAT-EYE LOOK

LIPS ARE RED OR BRIGHT PINK; CAN BE MATTE OR GLOSSY.

CURVE-CONSCIOUS CLOTHING

GLAMOROUS MANICURE (PREFERABLY RED)

HIGH HEELS TO ACCENTUATE CURVES (GOOD LUCK WITH THE WALKING PART!)

The Bombshell look is about extreme, hyper-accentuated femininity: extra-red lips, extra-bright hair, extra-hourglass figure. It's also one of the most formulaic looks—inspired almost entirely by mid-20th-century Hollywood stars. Pictures of Marilyn as her pre-Bombshell self, **Norma Jean Mortenson**, remind us that underneath it all, the Bombshell is just a regular girl. But when she's in Bombshell garb, her playful, overt sexuality is instantly recognizable and sure to garner attention in any situation. This is a look to wear only if you want to be noticed.

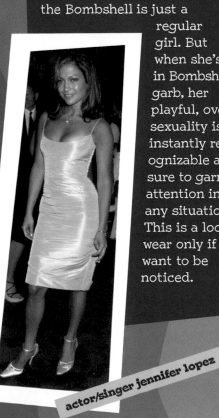

actor/singer jennifer lopez

ALSO TRY: PERFUME (SWEET, POWDERY SMELLS ARE VERY BOMBSHELL)

vamp goth

The Vamp, slang from the word "vampire," is a woman who uses her charm and beauty to seduce men and lead them to their ruin. Vamps are associated with vampires and other undead creatures, and part of the look's appeal is rooted in the human fascination with death. Today's Vamps are often known as Goths—probably due to gothic literature's emphasis on ghoulish stories—but the vamp persona has been around since ancient times.

In Greek mythology, the legendary Medusa was a beauty transformed into a monster with snakes for hair. One glance at her scary yet seductive face and men turned into stone.

Artist Edvard Munch used Medusa as a theme in his work, highlighting her seductiveness. The painting **Jealousy** (1896) shows a dark-haired, pale-skinned beauty entrapping a man with coils of her snakelike hair. Her large black lips and heavily accented eyes lure her victim in. These visual attributes—pale skin with darkly accented features—are signatures of the Vamp.

The original movie screen vamp was Theda Bara (born Theodosia Goodman). With roles like **Cleopatra** and **Salome**, she was an over-the-top seductress, playing up all that is dangerously sinful. Her skin was dramatically white, contrasting with her dark hair, lips, and eyes, always heavily rimmed with the sooty black of kohl.

Modern B-movie star Elvira is a campy goth Vamp. The self-declared "Mistress of the Dark" revels in all that's spooky. With her long black hair, heavily made-up eyes, deep red lips, and super-pale skin contrasting with tight black clothes, she looks like a sexy cartoon witch come to life.

Far less campy is the kind of darkly seductive appeal of singers like Siouxsie Sioux and Diamanda Galás. Sioux's pale, hollow-cheeked face, with black-rimmed eyes and lips, is almost a model for the Goth look. Galás, whose heritage is Greek, returns to the powerful Medusa prototype. She describes herself on stage as "witch, snake, vampire—whatever." Boys can go Goth too: Marilyn Manson's look is an androgynous twist on the Vamp/Goth style.

DARK HAIR (USUALLY DYED) BLACK OR DARK RED

HEAVY BLACK EYELINER CAN BE SMEARY— OR HARD-EDGED

ARTIFICIALLY PALE SKIN; CONTOUR IN CHEEK CREATES A HOLLOWING EFFECT.

BLACK VELVET, LEATHER, OR VINYL CHOKERS

DARK LIPS: CAN BE BLOODY RED, DEEP PURPLE, BLACK, OR ANOTHER DARK COLOR

LOTS OF HEAVY, LAYERED JEWELRY: SILVER, BEADS, MULTIPLE OR LARGE EARRINGS

LAYERS OF BLACK SHEER FABRICS; SHREDDED, TORN CLOTHING

LONG BLACK GLOVES (LONG BLACK FINGERNAILS UNDERNEATH)

SPIDERNET OR FISHNET STOCK-INGS, OR DARK PATTERNED TIGHTS

POINTY SHOES OR BOOTS

tv personality elvira

While the Vamp is often sexual and seductive, she may also have a touch of the melancholy romantic (think velvet, dried red roses, and candelabras). There are also Goths whose appeal is more cute than sexy. The woebegone damsels in **Edward Gorey**'s illustrations are more like child ghouls or gremlins than dangerous sex goddesses.

Vamp/Goth looks can range from slightly scary to truly terrifying. From the hypnotic, dangerous seductress to the innocuous witchypoo, this is a look for those who appreciate the dark side of beauty.

ALSO TRY: VINTAGE BLACK SLIPS; ANTIQUE MOURNING CLOTHING; ANYTHING WITH SKULLS, BATS, SPIDERWEBS, OR HALLOWEEN MOTIFS.

ice queen

The Ice Queen is the image of perfection associated most often with White Anglo-Saxon Protestant (WASP) aristocracy. The Ice Queen's look is about "good breeding." She wants to appear upper class, as if she were from a family with old money. There's nothing flamboyant about her. She exudes tasteful, understated wealth. Her clothes are expensive, cut with good, simple lines; they don't glitter or shine, or exhibit extremes of any kind. Her jewels are real but simple and delicate—a strand of pearls, tiny diamond studs, and a gold watch. The idea is that truly wealthy people don't need to show off with glitz; ostentation is tacky. (The Prep, who shares this philosophy, is the casual version of the Ice Queen.)

first lady jacqueline kennedy

There's a posture and demeanor that's essential to the look: while she may be friendly, the Ice Queen maintains a certain distance. Her reserved manner is in keeping with her understated fashion. She's cool and classy, as befits her name.

ICE QUEEN
IN ACTION

Katherine Hepburn in **The Philadelphia Story** (1940)

Grace Kelly in **Rear Window** (1954) and other 50s classics

Catherine Deneuve in **Belle De Jour** (1967)

Princess Diana

Vanessa Williams in **Soul Food** (1997)

Gwyneth Paltrow in **The Talented Mr. Ripley** (1999)

Lucy Liu in TV's **Ally McBeal** (1998–2002)

actor grace kelly

Grace Kelly was the quintessential Ice Queen, both on and offscreen—the coolly elegant movie star who became real-life royalty when she married Prince Rainier III of Monaco in 1956. Director Alfred Hitchcock called the blonde beauty a "snow-covered volcano," referring to the tension between her outer cool and inner fire. **Gwyneth Paltrow**'s Park Avenue polish has inspired some to consider her a modern-day model.

Because of their association with blondness and coldness, two classic Ice Queen qualities, Nordic women are often perceived to be Ice Queens. But Ice Queens don't have to be blond, or WASPs for that matter. **Lucy Liu** projected a kind of Ice Queen image as the chilly Ling Woo in the TV series **Ally McBeal**. And Miss America-turned-star **Vanessa Williams** cultivates a cool glamour both on screen and off.

During her years as First Lady in the early 1960s, **Jacqueline Kennedy** (later Onassis) reigned as the style queen of America in her pillbox hats and Chanel suits. **Women's Wear Daily** credited the former debutante with doing "more to uplift taste levels in the United States than any other woman." Though she was followed everywhere by photographers, she managed to hide strong feelings from the camera—most notably, after the assassination of her husband, President John F. Kennedy, in 1963. Jackie O, as she was later known, with her quiet voice and quiet style, oozed "class."

The Ice Queen is the epitome of upper-crust beauty. High-quality breeding may be hard to come by, but high-quality clothing can be bought—and a cool, calm, and classy attitude is free for anyone who wants to act the part.

THE ICE QUEEN'S BEAUTY LOOKS EFFORTLESS, BUT IMPECCABLE GROOMING IS KEY.

PERFECTLY STRAIGHT, SLEEK HAIR: IF YOU DON'T HAVE STRAIGHT HAIR, YOU WILL NEED A FLAT IRON FOR THIS LOOK. OR PULL HAIR BACK INTO A NEAT BUN.

MAKEUP IS MINIMAL: TINTED MOISTURIZER, A HINT OF MASCARA, AND NATURAL CHEEK AND LIP COLOR.

SIMPLE DIAMONDS OR PEARLS (FAKE CAN WORK)

A TOUCH OF MINK

CLASSIC CLOTHING, EXPENSIVE CUTS, A-LINE DRESSES

SMALL PURSE

SHORT OVAL, NATURAL NAIL— LIGHT COLOR OR FRENCH MANICURE

SIMPLE, LOW-HEELED PUMPS OR FLATS

ALSO TRY: VINTAGE 50S DRESSES OR SUITS, OR ADOPT A MORE CASUAL PREPPY ICE QUEEN LOOK WITH POLO SHIRTS AND KHAKIS

mod/new wave

"Mod" is short for "Modern." In 1960s England, the birthplace of Mod style, the burning question for teens was "Are you a Mod or a Rocker?" The Mods viewed the Rockers, leather-wearing descendants of 1950s country-influenced rock-and-roll, as old-schoolers who lived in the past and were an obstruction to the future.

judy jetson

The Mods were about modernism, change, and constant evolution. Mods had a new, clean-looking, minimalist aesthetic that incorporated space-age style with a touch of 1950s beatnik. Mod style had a strong effect on all design, not just fashion—furniture, appliances, textiles, even telephones of the day show a strong Mod aesthetic. The Vespa scooter was the quintessential Mod form of transportation.

The excitement of the space race, leading up to the walk on the moon in 1969, had a huge influence on the evolution of Mod fashion. Clothes were "aerodynamic," plastic and vinyl became fabrics of choice, and outfits had clear-cut lines and cut-away half-circles preparing the way for the trip into a new world and age. Makeup was stark and stylized: white shadow, pale lipstick, and sharp, black slashes of eyeliner. Hair was teased, sprayed, and hardened into "futuristic" styles.

MOD/NEW WAVE
IN ACTION

Marlo Thomas in TV's **That Girl** (1966–1971)

Pam Grier in 70s Blaxploitation films such as **Coffy** (1973)

Poly Styrene of X-ray Spex on album **Germfree Adolescents** (1978)

Mods in the film **Quadrophenia** (1979)

Elizabeth Hurley in **Austin Powers** (1997) and **Heather Graham** in **The Spy Who Shagged Me** (1999)

Influenced by op art (art using optical illusions), Rudi Gernreich paired various black-and-white check patterns in eye-dizzying fashion. The House of Courrèges was known for its white and silver space age aesthetic. Artist Piet Mondrian's simplified red, blue, and yellow geometric color scheme also shows up in Mod fashion.

Mods exported their look to America via designers like **Mary Quant** and on the backs of models such as **Twiggy** and **Jean Shrimpton**. The Mod face also crossed the Atlantic: light, frosty lipstick and wide, doll-like eyes (achieved by using fake lashes and/or gobs of mascara) were the tell-tale features.

New Wave music triggered an 80s Mod revival, with scooters and white vinyl boots making a comeback. Eighties Mods were more about kitsch and retro-ridiculousness, as modeled by major New Wave style-setters the **B-52s**. The girls in the group—**Kate Pierson** and **Cindy Wilson**—sported the namesake beehive do and thrift store versions of Mod fashions. Other 80s bands worked the minimal Mod look with asymmetrical haircuts and metallic, plastic, and otherwise futuristic clothing. The look has been revisited by musicians and fashion designers in recent years, too.

kate and cindy of the b-52s

Ultimately, Mod fashion, whether in its roots or in its more recent retro incarnations, is about a certain idea of modernity—a sleek, fashionable future world where every angle is designed just so, and not a hair is out of place. Today's Mod is simultaneously futuristic and retro, and has fun with the irony of this stylized (and perpetually stylish) vision of the future.

AN EVER-COOL LOOK THAT'S BOTH RETRO AND MODERN.

ANY 60S-INSPIRED HAIRSTYLE; IRONED HAIR OR HAIR THAT IS HIGH ON THE CROWN ALWAYS WORKS. TRY TEASING OR BACK-COMBING YOUR HAIR TO CREATE HEIGHT. LEAVE A LAYER OF UNTEASED HAIR ON TOP TO COVER THE TEASED PART—THIS CREATES A NEAT, SMOOTH SURFACE THAT LOOKS PUFFY RATHER THAN NESTY!

LIPSTICK IS LIGHT: NUDE TONES, FROSTS, OR EVEN OPAQUE LIGHT COLORS (WHITE, AT MOST EXTREME). TRY WEARING A FROSTED GLOSS ON TOP OF A COLOR YOU LIKE FOR A SOFTER VERSION OF THE MOD LIP.

EYES CAN BE CATLIKE WITH BLACK EYELINER OR HUGE AND WIDE-OPEN-LOOKING, WITH LIGHT OR BRIGHT SHADOWS AND SUPER-HEAVY LASHES.

A-LINE (TRIANGLE CUT)

MINISKIRTS ARE A CLASSIC MOD LOOK.

SUPER-GRAPHIC, BOLD PATTERNS. BRIGHT COLORS, BLACK AND WHITE OP ART PRINTS OR SWIRLY EMILIO PUCCI-STYLE PRINTS WORK TOO.

GO-GO BOOTS ARE A MOD STAPLE AND HAVE INFLUENCED MANY MODERN BOOT STYLES.

ALSO TRY: PLASTIC JEWELRY, VINYL ACCESSORIES, PATTERNED TIGHTS, JUMPSUITS OR LONG SLIM DRESSES

baby doll

"Sugar and spice and everything nice—that's what little girls are made of." All little girls are Baby Dolls at
some point—the stereotypical outfit for christenings,
first communions, and other childhood milestones
is the dressed-up Baby Doll in a lace dress,
tights, and Mary Janes. The playground
version might incorporate sturdier fabrics—
cotton or corduroy—with the same
empire waistline and heartier ruffles.

sue lyon in lolita

carroll baker in baby doll (1956)

Some people leave the Baby Doll
behind as they grow up, while some
mature Baby Dolls work the look to
their own advantage. The Baby Doll is
about insouciant innocence, a sweet
tooth, and being pretty. And on a girl
who's past the point of wearing the look
because her mother dressed her, it can
be about something else—sexiness.

Japanese society fetishizes Baby Dolls, and there are thousands of magazines (and websites) featuring very young
women in short dresses looking as innocent as possible.
Some of the look of the Japanese schoolgirl has come back
to us with global rave culture, where some kids sport paci-
fiers or candy jewelry and wear childish clothes.

BABY DOLL
IN ACTION

Brooke Shields in *Pretty
Baby* (1978)

Juliette Lewis in *Cape Fear*
(1991) and *Husbands and Wives*
(1992)

Courtney Love on Hole's
album *Pretty on the Inside*
(1991)

Shonen Knife (Japanese
Baby Doll band) on their *Let's
Knife* album (1993)

The sexiness of some Baby Dolls may be accidental—but there
is also a Baby Doll who is very knowingly using her innocent
look to entice. The classic sexy Baby Doll is Vladimir
Nabokov's character **Lolita**. In Nabokov's novel, an older man's
sexual obsession with a young girl results in a mutually
exploitative relationship. The book has been brought to the
screen twice, in 1962 and 1997. Both projects resulted in cen-
sorship and scandal—the already controversial relationship is
heightened by the fact that the older man in this case is married to the young girl's mother. "Lolita" has come to mean a
young girl who "seduces" an older man.

Courtney Love's famous "kinderwhore" look from her early rock career was an ironic take on this—she was obviously a grown woman but took on the fashion of a Baby Doll, upping it to a new level by smearing her makeup and tearing her pretty-little-girl dresses. She was the dirty Baby Doll, cast off in the corner but rising again to challenge those who dared to see her as helpless.

Babies need to be taken care of, and the Baby Doll look signals a certain dependence and need for approval from authority figures. Wearing it past a certain age can go beyond sassy and into sad or scary. In the film **Whatever Happened to Baby Jane?**, for example, a former child star clings to her youthful persona, with grotesque results. But in our youth-loving culture, the Baby Doll look wins plenty of admirers—and can be lots of fun. Just don't take candy from strangers...

CLEAN, SHINY HAIR WORN IN PIGTAILS, PONYTAIL, OR WITH BARRETTES. BANGS ARE ALSO BABY DOLL.

ROSY CHEEKS AND DEWY SKIN; SUBTLE GLITTER MAKEUP WORKS TOO.

PINK LIPS OR CLEAR LIP GLOSS

CURLED EYE-LASHES; MASCARA CAN BE APPLIED MORE HEAVILY IN THE CENTER TO GIVE THE IMPRESSION OF A ROUND EYE.

EMPIRE-WAIST BABY DOLL DRESSES

KIDS' AND/OR PLASTIC JEWELRY; CHARM BRACELETS

PINK OR PASTEL GLITTER NAIL POLISH

OVER-THE-KNEE SOCKS (FOR A SEXY BABY DOLL), OR TRY ANKLETS, KNEESOCKS, EVEN TIGHTS.

LUNCHBOX PURSE

MARY JANES OR SADDLE SHOES

ALSO TRY: CANDY JEWELRY, BLOOMERS, ANYTHING WITH HEARTS AND FLOWERS ON IT

bad girl

The Bad Girl believes that rules are made to be broken, whether it's rules about how to behave or how to dress. Pre-20th-century Bad Girls often acted out by donning men's clothes like the Androgyne, but since the start of the 20th century, being a Bad Girl has gone beyond gender-bending.

SEE PAGE 114 FOR A LOOK AT ANDROGYNES.

actor angelina jolie

"Wild West" lore is full of Bad Girl images. In the late 1870s, dime novels regaled readers with the fearless exploits of the sharpshooting **Calamity Jane**. Jane was flamboyant, occasionally dressed as a man, drove her own ox team (complete with whip), frequented saloons, and reputedly had a colorful vocabulary.

More recently, rock-and-roll became a new frontier for the Bad Girl, and helped define her modern image. Standing in front of a crowd with a guitar and a who-cares attitude became the modern equivalent of big guns and bad-ass rebellion. Rock's pioneering women were taking on a very boy-heavy rock scene, and part of the Bad Girl look evolved in response. Bad Girls are tough—intimidating, and unwilling to submit to authority. The Bad Girl look is sexy, both because it's overtly rebellious and because it sometimes means wearing clothes that have sexual (even fetishy) associations.

BAD GIRL
IN ACTION

Bonnie Parker, the 30s outlaw played by **Faye Dunaway** in **Bonnie and Clyde** (1967)

Joan Crawford in **Johnny Guitar** (1954)

Black Panther **Angela Davis**

Chrissie Hynde of **The Pretenders**

Patti Smith on album **Horses** (1975)

Tina Turner on album **Private Dancer** (1984)

TV sisters **Pinky and Leather Tuscadero** from **Happy Days** (1974–84)

Black leather has long been part of the Bad Girl uniform. When 60s pop stars **Marianne Faithfull** and **Brigitte Bardot** wanted to take on the Bad Girl image, they wore skintight leather outfits on camera. Before the leather-jacket look became popular, black leather was seen mostly in sex shops or on motorcycles—far outside the mainstream in either case. By taking on these outsider uniforms; the Bad Girl made it clear that she was a rebel, with or without a cause.

THIS IS A REBEL LOOK—NOT TOO PULLED TOGETHER.

MESSY, UNGROOMED HAIR—SPIKY OR STRINGY LAYERS, CHOPPY CUTS, HAIR IN THE EYES

DARK SMOKY EYES. USE BLACK EYELINER AND LOTS OF MASCARA (CAN BE MESSY FOR A REALLY BAD GIRL.)

TATTOO IS OPTIONAL

BLACK LEATHER JACKET

TANK TOPS, MUSCLE TEES , RIPPED CLOTHES

LEATHER PANTS OR JEANS

HIGH HEELED, OR CHUNKY MOTORCYCLE BOOTS

Rock (especially punk and metal) is still a driving force behind the Bad Girl look. But you don't have to be in head-to-toe chains and leather to be a Bad Girl. Just one accessory—some fishnets or motorcycle boots—can let the world know that you've got a touch of the rebel in you. Heavy black eyeliner or anything made out of black leather (a jacket, skirt, pants—even a cuff) will help you look the part—but when it comes down to it, what really makes a Bad Girl is her inner rebel shining through. A Bad Girl isn't satisfied with the way things are, wants you to know about it—and isn't afraid to wreak a little havoc along the way.

ALSO TRY: BLEACHED HAIR WITH ROOTS SHOWING; SHORT SKIRTS, FISHNETS

diva

rapper lil' kim

"Diva" comes from the Latin word for goddess. The Diva type takes that idea to heart and expects respect for her divinity (or else). Like many looks, Diva is as much an attitude as a matter of style.

The look is high maintenance, but the very essence of a Diva is the phrase "I'm worth it." Divas want to look well taken care of, because Divas like to be well taken care of. As far as fashion goes, this attitude translates into anything that looks obviously expensive. A Diva might change her style a bit after studying the latest fashion magazine, but the essential message is label-conscious, pampered, and ready for her close-up.

DIVA
IN ACTION

Opera singer **Maria Callas**

PERFORMING STARS:

Diana Ross

Barbra Streisand

Whitney Houston

Mary J. Blige

Jennifer Lopez

ACTORS:

Joan Collins

Susan Lucci as **Erica Kane** on **All My Children**

The original modern Divas were stars of stage and screen, and the word "diva" is still most closely associated with powerful female singers, from opera to pop to hip-hop. Many hip-hop Divas work a glam "ghetto fabulous" look with outsize jewelry and a haute street sensibility. Onstage, Divas often look like over-the-top showgirls, turning up the glitz and glitter, but always in high style. The Diva wants to ensure she's the center of attention, and that desire gets kicked up a notch when there's more attention to be had. Check out the red carpet at any Hollywood awards show for a reliable display of Diva-ness. **Diana Ross** was the Diva prototype at the 1972 Academy Awards, appearing as an Oscar nominee for playing tragic jazz Diva Billie Holiday (in a fabulously glam gown from Diva designer Bob Mackie). Decked out in their choice of gowns loaned by designers anxious to put their creations in the limelight, 21st-century Divas carry on the tradition, turning entertainment awards into fashion Diva contests.

model naomi campbell

The Diva likes to display the newest, lux-est, most of-the-moment fashion "do," and she's willing to go through a whole lot of effort to get herself there. If there's a fashion must-have, the Diva must have it—the salespeople at Gucci and Prada know her name, even if she isn't famous. Divas who can afford it often employ a whole entourage to help keep themselves fluffed up. A Diva has no problem wearing the highest heels—she doesn't walk anywhere. Her teeny bejeweled purse is just big enough for her cell phone, lipstick, and maybe some mad money. If she needs anything else, she can count on one of her admirers to fetch it from the limo—or from halfway around the world, if he has to. Everyone the Diva knows loves her. That's because if you don't love her, she doesn't want to know you.

singer mariah carey

PREENED TO PERFECTION; EVERY HAIR IN PLACE

SUNGLASSES

OF-THE-MOMENT MAKEUP, PERFECTLY APPLIED

SERIOUS JEWELRY (AT LEAST LOOKS LIKE IT COSTS $$$$)

PERFECT MANICURE— LONG NAILS

THE PERFECT (PRICEY) PURSE— JUST ENOUGH ROOM FOR LOGOS

ALSO TRY: STRAIGHTENED HAIR, LOTS OF GOLD AND SPARKLY JEWELRY, LOGOWEAR, AND FUR

SUPER-HIGH HEELS (NO NEED TO WALK)

gamine

The term "gamine" comes from the French word for "street kid." It calls to mind urchins—impish adolescents who somehow possess oodles of style. Gamines generally sport super-short hair, often layered so it conveys a slightly tousled feel, hinting at a little devil wild streak. It's called a pixie cut. The quintessential Gamine reflects the urban flair of Paris, although she can live anywhere. The Gamine often looks boyish—exuding the Peter Pan "I won't grow up" spirit—but she's definitely a girl. The combination of the tough and vulnerable, along with her youthful, playful style, is what has given the Gamine such enduring appeal.

GAMINE
IN ACTION

Audrey Hepburn in **Sabrina** (1954), **Breakfast at Tiffany's** (1961), and other films

Jean Seberg in **Bonjour, Tristesse** (1958) and **Breathless** (1959)

60s model **Twiggy**

Mia Farrow in **Rosemary's Baby** (1968)

Winona Ryder in **Little Women** (1994) and in **Girl, Interrupted** (1999)

Anita Mui in **Rumble in the Bronx** (1996)

Actor **Jada Pinkett Smith**

Paulette Goddard was the original American Gamine in **Modern Times** (1936), her most famous film with frequent costar and eventual husband Charlie Chaplin. Almost unbearably petite, she's more than capable—stealing bananas on the waterfront and handing them out to her fellow urchins.

actor audrey hepburn

In the 50s and early 60s **Audrey Hepburn**, the ultimate Gamine, added a couture touch to the urchin sensibility. Thin and flat-chested, she wore Givenchy almost exclusively and became a style-setter whose influence is still felt today. Hepburn's chic short hair and doe eyes captivated an American public whose other icon at the time was Marilyn Monroe. Her characters sparkled with mischief, notably as a spunky runaway princess-in-disguise in **Roman Holiday** (1953). In **Funny Face** (1957), she played a beatnik, jazzy Gamine. The short pixie haircut was the look of choice among **beatnik*** girls in the 1950s.

While Hepburn played with glamour, actress **Jean Seberg** kept her Gamine look close to its urchin roots. Small-boned, Bambi-eyed, and short-haired, Jean Seberg was the pert yet inscrutable sidekick of the ultra-cool-looking thug played by Jean-Paul Belmondo in **Breathless**. Seberg's striped boat-neck shirt and tight, cropped pants are a staple of Gamine style even today.

SHORT AND SLEEK OR SHORT AND TOUSLED. SHORT HAIR IS PART OF THE GAMINE LOOK—IF YOUR HAIR IS LONG, PULL IT BACK AS NEATLY AS YOU CAN.

MINIMAL MAKEUP: CLEAR SKIN, FLUSHED CHEEKS, AND MASCARA ON THE OUTSIDE UPPER LASHES

NO JEWELRY

THE BLUE AND WHITE STRIPED BOAT-NECK TOP IS A CLASSIC GAMINE STAPLE.

CROPPED PANTS, BOY-CUT CLOTHES, PREP-SCHOOL LOOKS

SIMPLE, SLIM-FITTING CLOTHING

BALLET FLATS OR CANVAS SNEAKERS

jean seberg in *breathless*

The early 90s saw a Gamine variation termed "the waif," but these lank, sullen, long-haired girls had little in common with the bright, energetic vibe of the true Gamine.

The Gamine look today isn't limited to girls who look like little boys. Aspects of the Gamine look can be adopted by any girl, especially if she has a tousled short haircut. Striped sailor fashions, cropped boy-cut pants, and flats give everyone a touch of the Gamine—as does an impish attitude!

*beatnik The beatniks or Beats, were the pre-mod, pre-hippie bohemians of the late 50s and early 60s. Associated with philosophy, jazz, and cafes (either Parisian Left Bank or New York's Greenwich Village), the Beats were bookish but brazen. They wore minimalist black clothing—leotards or turtlenecks, with straight skirts or slim pants—stereotypically topped off by a black beret.

ALSO TRY: NAUTICAL LOOKS, KNEE-LENGTH SKIRTS

goddess

The Goddess is a woman who revels in her body. There is power in her womanly curves, and she believes in showing them off. In ancient Greece and many other cultures, representations of goddesses portrayed strong women with abundant curves. Emphasizing the fertility and regenerative abilities of women, these paintings and sculptures often depicted goddesses of earth and grain—but statuesque, shapely figures were seen in many images of women.

actor catherine zeta-jones

Peter Paul Rubens (1577-1640) was a Flemish painter of primarily religious subjects and society portraits. His lush, unabashed portrayals of flesh (both male and female) were so powerful that even now we call voluptuous women "Rubenesque."

FOR MORE ON RUBENS, SEE PAGE 12

There's an almost overwhelming sensuality to this look. In paintings, the Goddess is often pictured surrounded by sensory pleasures. The overtones of fertility are unmistakable. The Goddess flaunts a body that was clearly designed to bear and nurture children.

GODDESS
IN ACTION

Lillian Russell in **Wildfire** (1915)

Mae West in **I'm No Angel** (1933) and other 30s hits

Anna Magnani in **The Rose Tattoo** (1955)

Elizabeth Taylor in **Taming of the Shrew** (1967)

Kate Winslet in **Titanic** (1997)

Catherine Zeta-Jones in **The Mask of Zorro** (1998)

Amisha Patel in **Badri** (2000)

Nigella Lawson in the TV show **Nigella Bites**

Singer **Jill Scott**

actor lisa nicole carson

The Goddess look doesn't require a full figure (though it's a great look for a girl or woman who has one). Whether a Goddess has curves in just a few places or all over, her look is about making the most of her shape. Curves are part of what distinguishes women's bodies from men's, and the goddess wants that distinction to be immediately apparent. Everything about her plays up the natural power of the female: she's strong but soft.

Today's Goddess style refers back to that of her forerunners. She may even wear clothing inspired by classical Greco-Roman goddess-wear: wraps, draping, and empire waists emphasize her imposing physique. She loves clothing cut on the bias (so that the fabric hangs diagonally on her body, highlighting her shape) and gauzy layers of soft, flowing fabrics such as silk or velvet.

There is a definite air of defiance to a modern Goddess—she is about celebrating the beauty of the body, not starving it into submission. She has plentiful curves and doesn't apologize for them (in opposition to the thin-is-in aesthetic). Her look emphasizes ultra femininity and sexuality, as well as a strong sense of self-worth. The Goddess embodies joie de vivre, sensuality, and above all, pleasure.

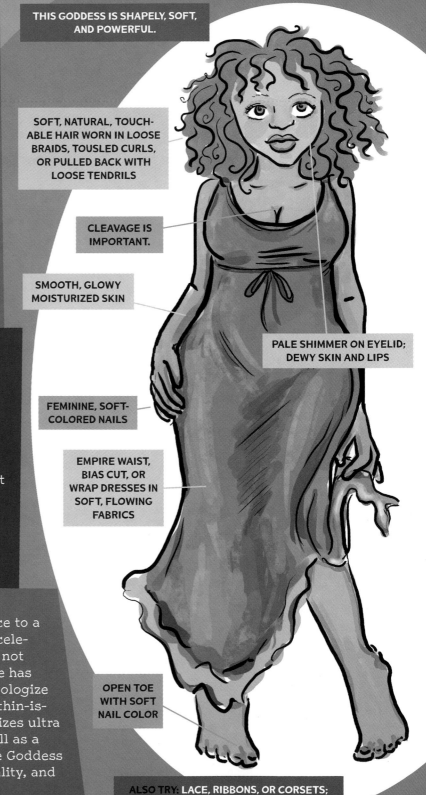

THIS GODDESS IS SHAPELY, SOFT, AND POWERFUL.

SOFT, NATURAL, TOUCH-ABLE HAIR WORN IN LOOSE BRAIDS, TOUSLED CURLS, OR PULLED BACK WITH LOOSE TENDRILS

CLEAVAGE IS IMPORTANT.

SMOOTH, GLOWY MOISTURIZED SKIN

PALE SHIMMER ON EYELID; DEWY SKIN AND LIPS

FEMININE, SOFT-COLORED NAILS

EMPIRE WAIST, BIAS CUT, OR WRAP DRESSES IN SOFT, FLOWING FABRICS

OPEN TOE WITH SOFT NAIL COLOR

ALSO TRY: LACE, RIBBONS, OR CORSETS; VISIBLE SLIPS OR BRA STRAPS

it girl/flapper

The original 1920s Flapper look was in every way a rebellion against past standards of ladylike beauty. Fashions were inspired by freedom, shedding the corsets and cumbersome layers of skirts for a new slim silhouette that emphasized narrow hips and a boyish physique as opposed to the traditional hourglass. Hemlines rose to near the knee, freeing the legs. Finally, women could really kick up their heels and dance to the Jazz revolution, flapping their way through the Charleston. (This emphasis on slender bodies created its own restrictions, however, and women who weren't naturally flat-chested bound their boobs to try to achieve the straight line required by fashion.)

actor louise brooks

IT GIRL/FLAPPER
IN ACTION

Clara Bow in **It** (1927)

Josephine Baker in French 20s films such as **La Revue des Revues** (1927)

Louise Brooks in **Pandora's Box** (1928) and other 20s films

Julie Andrews in **Thoroughly Modern Millie** (1967)

Mia Farrow in **The Great Gatsby** (1974)

Kirsten Dunst in **The Cat's Meow** (2002)

One of the definining traits of the Flapper was her modern haircut—a short, easy-to-care-for "bob," often with bangs. Trend-setting fashion designer **Coco Chanel** was one of the first to bob her hair in 1917. Hair was the crowning glory in the traditional image of womanhood, and cutting it off sent a powerful message of youth and rebellion. Further defying convention, Flappers wore lipstick, which had previously been reserved for "painted ladies" and prostitutes. Their behavior was similarly rebellious: they smoked cigarettes and drove their own cars (prior to then wealthy women were almost always chauffeured by men). The 20s also brought more economic independence to the many women who entered the workforce for the first time (often as salesgirls and secretaries).

two flappers dancing the charleston

In the eyes of the public, the ultimate Flapper was **Clara Bow**. After starring in the 1927 silent film **It**, she became known as the "It Girl." With her impish good looks and cupid's bow pout, this saucy, fun-loving girl definitely had "it"—sex appeal.

THE FLAPPER LOOK IS A PARTY-GIRL CLASSIC. MODERN "IT" GIRLS CAN TRANSLATE THE SPIRIT INTO THEIR OWN STYLE.

Louise Brooks, known as "The Girl with the Black Helmet" for her bobbed hairstyle, also had "it." Her sassy, flirtatious style stole men's hearts in 1920s Flapper comedies as well as in more serious European films. **Josephine Baker**, the first black American star, flaunted "it" all over Europe in extraordinary beaded gowns that highlighted her incredible dancing.

Flapper style will always carry the connotation of fun-loving rebellion. But the idea of the It Girl extends beyond fashion. A devil-may-care attitude and a love of dancing, parties, and nightlife are timeless It Girl traits. Modern girls who make their mark in the public eye carry the Flapper spirit (if not the tell-tale bob), and the ever-evolving idea of "it" into the future.

BOBBED HAIR IS PRETTY MUCH A DEFINING ELEMENT OF THE FLAPPER LOOK. THE CLASSIC VERSION IS STRAIGHT WITH SHORT BANGS. BUT CURLY HAIR OR NO BANGS WORK TOO. WHAT DEFINES A BOB IS THE LENGTH THAT FALLS BETWEEN THE EAR AND THE SHOULDER.

21ST-CENTURY FLAPPERS NEED NOT FEEL COMPELLED TO BIND THEIR BOOBS. (IF YOU'RE WELL-ENDOWED AND LOOKING TO FLATTEN THINGS OUT, TRY A TRUSTY SPORTS BRA!)

PEARLS ARE BIG: LONG STRANDS, SHORT CHOKERS, OR BOTH. LONG BEADED NECKLACES ARE GOOD TOO.

COCKTAIL DRESSES ARE ALWAYS PARTY-READY. SLEEVELESS STYLES ARE FLIRTIEST.

CLOSED-TOE SHOES— A BUCKLE OR MARY JANE STYLE IS VERY FLAPPER.

THE FACE IS A BIT PAINTED: DARK EYELINER AND MASCARA AND STRONG RED LIPS.

GLOVES (LONG OR SHORT)

SMALL CLUTCH

THE DROP WAIST WAS A REVOLUTION OF THE FLAPPER AGE. IT'S STILL A FUN AND FLATTERING LOOK.

RETRO-LOOKING HOSIERY (TINY FISHNETS, SEAMED STOCKINGS)

ALSO TRY: FRINGE, 80S RETRO DROP-WAIST COCKTAIL DRESSES (FROM THRIFT STORES)

androgyne

an•drog•y•nous

1 : displays the characteristics or nature of both male and female
2 a : neither specifically feminine nor masculine
  b : suited for either sex
3 : obscures or reverses traditional male and female roles

Whether the Androgyne look is about obscuring the distinction between male and female or adopting the look of the opposite gender, it's always about playing with traditional gender roles.

Some women simply like the aesthetic or comfort of men's clothing; others use the fashion statement to express an identity that exists outside the realm of traditional male and female roles; still others identify more with maleness than with femaleness.

actor marlene dietrich

ANDROGYNE
IN ACTION

Marlene Dietrich in **The Blue Angel** (1930) and other 30s classics

Greta Garbo in **Queen Christina** (1933)

Katharine Hepburn in **Sylvia Scarlett** (1936)

Diane Keaton in **Annie Hall** (1977)

Tilda Swinton in **Orlando** (1993)

Mulan, in Disney's **Mulan** (1998)

MUSICANS/PERFORMERS **Grace Jones**, **k.d. lang**, **Annie Lennox**, **Patti Smith**

SEE CROSS-DRESSING ON PAGE 117

In the distant past, when women's roles were greatly restricted, dressing as a man was a route to freedom. As women from Civil War enlistee **Sarah Emma Edmonds** to stagecoach driver **Charlotte (Charley) Parkhurst** discovered, women disguised as men could gain access to places they were forbidden from going. They could also gain authority and power. For these reasons, certain female artists and writers have sometimes taken on androgynous guises. One of the most famous Androgynes in history was the 19th-century French author **George Sand**, who took a man's name in creating her quasi-male identity. Although she dressed in men's attire, she was considered extremely seductive and had liaisons with many of the most creative men of her time.

Many creative women since then, especially musicians, have worked the Androgyne look to make powerful statements with their public personas. Of course, it's not necessary to be an artist to experiment with androgyny. Lots of girls who identify as "tomboys" early on understand the freedom, ease, and sense of power that comes with adopting some boy style and attitude.

The Androgyne is a look that challenges expectations and makes its own definitions. It can be a playful tease about how we present ourselves or a necessary expression of a feeling of difference. Whatever the reasons behind androgynous dressing, it's a style that has an impact on people. Some people find playing with gender roles disturbing and repellent, while others find it utterly compelling. It's this push and pull of opposite forces that gives the Androgyne her power.

ACCENTUATING THE BROWS GIVES YOUR FACE A MANNISH TOUCH.

SHORT HAIR, FROM A BASIC BOY-CUT TO A MORE MESSY SHAG, TO A RETRO POM-PADOUR OR FLAT-TOP. A CREW CUT IS THE MOST SEVERE OPTION.

DOWNPLAY THE LIPS BY USING A NUDE LIPCOLOR, POWDER OR FOUNDATION, OR NO LIPCOLOR AT ALL. MAKEUP IN GENERAL PLAYS UP YOUR FEMININE FEATURES.

LONG HAIR CAN ALSO WORK IF YOU SLICK IT BACK, IRON IT STRAIGHT AND SEVERE, OR LAYER IT FOR A ROCK-AND-ROLL ANDROGYNE LOOK.

OXFORD CLOTH SHIRTS AND TIES

MEN'S (OR BOYS') SUITS, KHAKIS, OR JEANS

MEN'S-STYLE SHOES: OXFORDS, BUCKS, OR LOAFERS

ALSO TRY: ANY MEN'S-STYLE CLOTHES. THRIFT STORES ARE A GOLD-MINE FOR THIS LOOK! TRY THE BOYS' SECTION IF YOU'RE SMALL.

SCREEN ANDROGYNES

Throughout the history of cinema, there have been countless examples of women taking on men's style. The first half of the 20th century saw movie stars like **Greta Garbo**, **Marlene Dietrich**, and **Katharine Hepburn** crossing the fashion threshold by combining feminine poise with masculine style. The actresses could often be found wearing pants (still unusual at the time) in their roles as well as their personal lives. (Marlene Dietrich famously owned ten pantsuits which were all she wore in public.) When Greta Garbo donned princely gear in **Queen Christina** or Marlene Dietrich put on her signature tux in **The Blue Angel** or **Morocco**, it added to the mystery of their allure—making us wonder if we could ever know (or control) them. The Androgyne refuses to be put in a category—even one as basic as gender.

In the film **Annie Hall**, **Diane Keaton** turned androgyny into a quirky, anticonventional statement. Nothing she wore quite fit; it was all oversize—which lent a casual, nonthreatening air to her character (and to those who imitated the look).

diane keaton in annie hall

singer k.d. lang

ANDROGYNE ROCKERS

Lots of women rockers have taken on the Androgyne as an act of rebellion, freedom, and power. In the 1970s groundbreaking rocker **Patti Smith** created her own androgynous style by adopting the tough fashion and stance previously associated with male rock stars.

Model/singer/performer **Grace Jones**, with her buzz-cut Afro and muscular, almost flat-chested body, challenged concepts of womanhood. And **Annie Lennox** of the Eurythmics deliberately played off of the gender-bending question behind androgyny—is it a man or a woman? With her bright orange crew cut and men's business suits, she disrupted notions and expectations about maleness and femaleness. In her "Love Is a Stranger" video, she keeps "changing" sexes, shifting costumes and wigs. "One of the main reasons I wear the clothes I do and have an androgynous image," Lennox explains, "is because I didn't want to be seen as a 'girlie' singer wearing pretty dresses. I don't want to change sexual labels—I want to sidestep them, and to confound people a little bit with something fresher and less clichéd."

Singer **k.d. lang** embodies a look that is more typically "masculine," tough, or "butch." Her mannish look was even more controversial in the world of country music, where traditional roles are the norm.

ANDROGYNY SWINGS BOTH WAYS

Skinny, sexually ambiguous glam rockers such as **David Bowie**, **Iggy Pop**, the **New York Dolls**, and **Alice Cooper** set the stage in the 60s and 70s for the 80s male Androgynes **Boy George**, **Michael Jackson**, and the artist who was then known as **Prince**. With platform heels, spandex, sequins, and sparkly eye shadow, these men oozed a new, undefinable kind of sexuality that appealed to (and was imitated by) boys and girls of every persuasion.

singer David Bowie (left) and his then-wife Angie

CROSS-DRESSING

When people dress completely in the guise of the opposite sex, it is called cross-dressing or sometimes, dressing in "drag." The idea of drag implies that the cross-dressing is clearly an act of artifice rather than total illusion. Drag queens, for example, often create caricatures of women, with extreme hair and makeup and a hyper-heightened sense of glamour. Drag kings take on extreme masculine clothing and demeanor, which often includes cultivated or artificial facial hair and fake "bulges." There is a performance-oriented aspect to drag, which may involve shows, or just showing off the persona.

Transvestites are people who attempt to actually be perceived as members of the opposite sex, although they retain the physical sex organs they were born with. Although many people assume that all cross-dressers are homosexuals, studies have actually shown that an equal number of heterosexuals engage in cross-dressing. The idea of gender identity is a complicated one, and while it may be tied to sexual orientation, it isn't always.

Cross-dressing can be a pastime or a way of life. For some people, it is a way of expressing what they feel is their true identity, trapped inside a body of the wrong gender. The film **Boys Don't Cry** (1999) told the true story of a girl who recreated herself as a boy to express her identity and sexuality (with tragic results).

BUTCH

The word "butch" was originally used in the 1950s to describe a lesbian woman who consciously took on the man's role in her romantic relationships with other women. This very specific use of the word has become outdated (as has the notion that there needs to be a man's role in a lesbian relationship). The word "butch" is now more widely used to describe any girl or woman (whatever her sexuality) who incorporates male attributes—attitude, short hair, or clothing—into her style, generally carrying a connotation of toughness.

TRANSSEXUALS

Transsexuals are men (or women) who have gone the extra step of physically altering their bodies to eliminate (or add) sex organs and shift their hormonal balance accordingly. After surgery and extensive treatments (hair removal and breast augmentation in the case of men; penile implants in the case of women), they grow to resemble the opposite sex in all ways, although they are incapable of bearing children.

bohemian/gypsy

"Bohemian" refers to people from a region called Bohemia in Czechoslovakia, but the term has come to be associated with vagabonds, especially Gypsies. The Gypsies are a nomadic people who originated in India but now live throughout Europe and Southwest Asia and refer to themselves as "Roma." In its modern usage, the word "Bohemian" refers to anyone living an unconventional lifestyle.

The Bohemian look is a reflection of this offbeat, artsy sensibility: the Bohemian likes to mix patterns; is fond of vibrant colors, embroidery, and fringe; and draws from a variety of peasant cultures.

actor lisa bonet

In the late 50s and early 60s haute couture designers such as Yves Saint Laurent brought the Gypsy look to the upper class with luxe peasant styling (embroidered velvet rather than cotton) and ethnic accessories. Later in the 1960s the Bohemian style segued into hippie fashion, joining a revolt against convention and the 1950s emphasis on getting ahead and fitting in with the crowd. The African American civil rights movement brought African touches—full afros and chunky beads—to the look. Bralessness signified the freedom ushered in by the women's rights movement. Some hippies went psychedelic, with tie-dyed clothes reflecting the trippy sensibility.

BOHEMIAN/GYPSY
IN ACTION

Artist **Frida Kahlo** (1907–1954)

Singer **Joni Mitchell**

Cher on 70s albums such as **Half-Breed** (1973)

Alanis Morrisette on album **Jagged Little Pill** (1995)

Kate Hudson in **Almost Famous** (2000)

India.Arie on album **Acoustic Soul** (2001)

Hair—whether it was wavy, stringy, or kinky—was worn "natural," free at last from the teasing, straightening, and over-styling of previous decades. **Sonny and Cher** were the ultimate Bohemian couple, with their long hair, fur vests, bell bottoms, and fringe.

Today's Bohemian can pick and choose from any of these influences and more. Bohemian girls can be barefoot or sandaled; with flowers, braids, or beads in their hair; wearing loose-fitting vintage dresses, layered Indian prints with jeans, or even good old tie-dye. They might be outdoorsy hippie girls who wear hiking boots with peasant skirts. Or they could be unconventional urban gypsies, like designer **Betsy Johnson**, who applies a bold palette and tighter fit to the Boho mix-and-match aesthetic.

Long, loose, unruly hair says Bohemian, as do ethnic accessories—whether they're Native American turquoise, colorful Indian beads, Gypsy hoop earrings, or Tibetan shawls. Since Gypsy fashions continue to influence haute couture designers, and authentic Gypsy-wear is affordable by nature, there is no shortage of looks available to Bohemians on any budget.

singer janis joplin

Bohemian/Gypsy is a look that's about keeping your options open. Anything goes!

CHEEK AND LIP COLORS IN BROWNS, RUSSETS, OR PURPLES FOR AN INTENSE LOOK

LONG, UNRULY HAIR. A MOP OF MESSY CURLS IS CLASSIC, BUT SHORT OR STRAIGHT HAIR CAN ALSO WORK IF IT'S UNKEMPT.

SMUDGY EYE MAKEUP IN BROWNS, MAROONS, AND DEEP PURPLES CREATES AN INTENSE GYPSY EYE. TRY LINING WITH BROWN KOHL, THEN SMUDGING WITH YOUR FINGERS.

ETHNIC JEWERY WITH LOTS OF STONES AND SILVER

PEASANT SHIRT, LAYERED LOOK

BROWN LEATHER OR SUEDE BELTS AND BAGS

BELL BOTTOMS, RIPPED JEANS, PEASANT SKIRTS, OR ANYTHING ASSOCIATED WITH "HIPPIE" FASHION CAN STILL CREATE A BOHEMIAN FEEL.

SANDALS CAN BE FLAT FOR EASE OF MOVEMENT OR HAVE HEELS FOR A FANCY, FASHION-Y BOHEMIAN LOOK.

ALSO TRY: EARTHY SCENTS. ESSENTIAL OILS LIKE PATCHOULI AND MUSK ARE VERY BOHO.

african queen

Befitting her royal position, the African Queen stands tall and proud, asserting her power with boldly colored fabrics, layers of vibrant beads or gleaming metals from brass to gold, and elaborate hairstyling. She comes from a long line of regal stunners, including **Queen Nefertiti** of Egypt (c. 1370 BCE) and the **Queen of Sheba** (Makeda), who reigned in Ethiopia in the 10th century BCE.

The African Queen comes from a tradition of respect for women, immortalized in sculptures like an early-16th-century bronze from Nigeria, which shows the Benin queen mother with her head held high, accentuated by a towering headdress. Her strength and capability are recorded in the tales of the warrior queens like **Amina**, a Zazzuan (Nigerian) conqueror in the late 16th century, and **Yaa Asantewaa**, who led the Ashanti people (in Ghana) in their fight against the British at the start of the 20th century.

queen nefertiti

AFRICAN QUEENS
IN ACTION

Models:

Iman

Roshumba

Alek Wek

Actor **Alfre Woodard**

Performing Artists:

Queen Latifah

Miriam Makeba

Les Nubians

Today in Africa, queenly magnificence is especially visible on ceremonial occasions. In Ghana, Ashanti women of noble birth wear the royal Kente cloth with its striking geometric patterns in brilliant oranges, reds, blues, greens, yellows, and black. Multiple chains and bracelets of gold adorn their necks, arms, and ankles. A young Maasai bride in Kenya is decked out in multicolored beaded glory. For her initiation into womanhood, a Ndebele girl in South Africa wears "golwani," beaded hoops, around her waist and legs, emphasizing her voluptuous shape. Outfits vibrate with strong color and lively graphic design. As the Turkana in northern Kenya say, "It's the things a woman wears that make her beautiful."

Spurred on by the civil rights movement of the 1950s and 60s, many African American women were drawn to African Queen style as an expression of self-respect. In America the African Queen proudly displays her heritage, wearing brightly hued Kente cloth with saturated colors or boldly patterned block-print African fabrics. Like the Ashanti royalty and the Fulani women of Mali, the American African Queen shows off wealth and status with her jewelry, with dangling earrings, bangled arms, and layered necklaces. Her hair is often her crowning glory, done up in a range of Afrocentric styles, from bantu knots to elaborate braided twists to beaded cornrows.

KOHL-RIMMED EYES, SHINY CHEEKS. LIPSTICK CAN BE DARK OR NATURAL.

HEAD WRAPS COVER DREADLOCKS, AFROS, OR BRAIDS.

LONG NECK ACCENTUATED WITH BOLD JEWELRY IN GOLD OR SILVER, BEADS, STONES, OR SHELLS

ARM JEWELRY

DARK, GLOWING SKIN

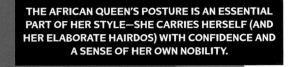

singer erykah badu

LONG, ELABORATELY DECORATED NAILS

CAFTANS OR TUNICS IN BRIGHT OR NATURAL COLORS

LEATHER SANDALS

ALSO TRY: BOLD PRINTS, WOVEN BAGS

121

futurebabe

The Futurebabe embodies our fantasies of what the future will look like. Her earliest incarnation was the space-age Mod, a look that had such an impact it's still around today. But while the Mod look sticks to its minimalist roots, this look is about taking on whatever form the fantastic future might bring and evolving the fashion accordingly. The Futurebabe is an early adopter of anything new, whether it's a fabric, style, color, or ideology. Lately, futurism has been about gadgets, computers, and a whimsical galactic sensibility.

SEE ALSO MOD ON PAGE 100

Science fiction, with its sometimes cartoony aesthetic, has created many iconic future girls. In the 70s Futurebabe **Jaime Sommers**, the Bionic Woman (played by Lindsay Wagner), combined technology with the earthy fashions of the time. She was a cyborg, with super-performing body parts (an ear, an arm, and both legs). Her descendants include other "enhanced" women like **Jessica Alba** on **Dark Angel** and the Bob Mackie-clad women of **Star Trek,** many of whom have special implants and powers, as well as a tendency to dress in form-fitting outfits.

fashions by tiyanon group

FUTUREBABE
IN ACTION

Women of **Star Trek**

Artist **Mariko Mori**

Milla Jovovich in **The Fifth Element** (1997)

Japanese virtual pop star **Kyoko Date**

Japanese girls in the book **Fruits** by photographer Shoichi Aoki (2002)

Animated characters **Aeon Flux** (MTV cartoon 1996–1997) and **Sailor Moon**

TLC in **"No Scrubs"** video (1995)

Bjork on album **Telegram** (1997)

Britney in **"Ooops... I did it again"** video (2000)

Cartoons, especially Japanese anime, provide some of the most colorful images of futurism, and the Futurebabe. The anime character **Sailor Moon** embraces the future with enthusiasm. Sailor favors bright form-fitting clothes with whimsical details. Her tiara is also a weapon. More serious Futurebabes from the world of anime include **Misato Katsuragi** and **Maya Ibuki** of the Neon Genesis Evangelion collective. Misato and Maya are scientists and their clothes reflect that function, with pockets for tools and built-in communication links. Futurebabes love gadgets—the more integrated, the better. The Futurebabe will be first in line for a cellphone–chip implant, but until then she'll settle for a camera watch.

performer nina hagen

Technology isn't just Futurebabe's friend in terms of gadgets and lifestyle—she takes advantage of it to play with her look too. She favors cutting-edge fabrics such as stretch leather and microfibers, and experimental designers who use lasers and reflective materials. Convertible clothing appeals to her, and her outfits often feature sleeves that can be snapped off and worn as gaiters, or a jacket that can be used as an umbrella in case of a sudden rainfall.

Techno music is the Futurebabe soundtrack. And rave culture's plastic-y, neon aesthetic is Futurebabe-inspired. Super-high platforms are a staple of the Futurebabe—as seen on the streets in Tokyo (Futurebabe central).

This girl loves to play with her hair color and texture, and often prefers it to look more cartoony than natural. There's a bit of the clown to the Futurebabe's look, and little kids tend to respond to her with delight. She takes this in stride—after all, she believes that children are our future.

HYPER-GIRLIE HAIR STYLES: POM-POMS, PIG-TAILS, OR AFRO PUFFS

ARTIFICIAL-LOOKING HAIR IN BRIGHT COLORS—TRY COLORED HAIRSPRAYS OR GELS.

SCI-FI MAKEUP: SILVER, NEON COLORS

GOGGLE-LIKE GLASSES

GADGETS, PLASTIC JEWELRY, AND CRAZY WATCHES

TIGHT-FITTING CLOTHING BUT NOT MUCH SKIN EXPOSED; FLUORESCENTS AND METALLICS

BOOTS/ GIANT PLATFORMS ARE A MUST

ALSO TRY: VINYL, BLINKING LIGHTS, REFLECTIVE CLOTHING, JUMPSUITS

power jock

The power jock is strong, athletic, and proud of her physical prowess. Her muscle-bearing, no-fuss style celebrates her physique and facilitates her athleticism, whatever her sport of choice.

the williams sisters

In ancient Greece, Power Jocks could be found competing in the Herean Games. At the time women were prohibited from participating in the men's Olympics, so they set up a competition of their own. The events ranged from chariot racing to wrestling, with women showing off their athletic prowess and their sheer determination.

Up until relatively recent times, women were thought to be too delicate and fragile to pursue sports and athletics. And where women did compete (in tennis and golf), they were strongly discouraged from appearing unladylike in dress.

POWER JOCK
IN ACTION

Jane Fonda in her 80s fitness books and videos

Linda Hamilton in **Terminator 2** (1991)

Lucy Lawless in TV's **Xena: Warrior Princess** (1995–1999)

Demi Moore in **Gi Jane** (1997)

Michelle Rodriguez in **Girlfight** (2000)

Boxer **Laila Ali**

Volleyball champ **Gabrielle Reece**

Tennis stars **Venus and Serena Williams**

The Power Jock really began to take hold after 1972 with the passing of Title IX, a law enacted by Congress that mandated equal funding for women's sports programs. The 1980s saw a boom in exercise videos, as women like **Jane Fonda** and **Olivia Newton-John** popularized "getting physical." The aerobics craze created a new fitness fashion, and since then, almost without exception, fashion has embraced a fit look as part of its ideal of beauty.

soccer champ brandi chastain

The emphasis in the Power Jock's appearance is on strength, athleticism, and freedom. She wants to be able to use her body at a moment's notice, without worrying about constricting her range of motion. Statement sneakers—the hippest brand or the latest in high-tech—and loose pants or Lycra leggings (depending on her style and sport) show that fitness is her priority.

Her clothing might highlight her body as a point of pride: crop tops, tanks, and other revealing clothing show the strength of her human machine and the hard work she puts into it. She usually wears short or pulled-back hair, and minimal makeup that won't run into her eyes when she sweats. But she may add some color or flair to her look—flashy hair accessories, Day-Glo spandex, or decorated nails—as a reminder to all that she's more than just a competitor...or perhaps it's just another intimidation tactic.

Not all Power Jocks are athletes. **Janet Jackson** and **Madonna** work the Power Jock look offstage, often sporting low-cut sweats and tiny tees, all abs and biceps. All it takes is a powerful body, and the attitude to go with it!

FUSS-FREE HAIR HOLDS UP TO SWEAT.

THE POWER JOCK PUTS TIME AND ENERGY INTO HER PHYSIQUE—AND IT SHOWS.

NATURAL FLUSH FROM EXERTION

MUSCLES GALORE

SWEAT-BANDS OR SPORT WATCHES

ABS-CONSCIOUS CLOTHING

LYCRA IS FABRIC OF CHOICE.

HOT-OFF-THE-ASSEMBLY-LINE SNEAKS

ALSO TRY: YOGA WEAR AND HOODED SWEATSHIRTS

125

california girl

The Beach Boys sang about an "Endless Summer" and the California Girl personifies it. She's clean-cut, sporty, and feminine. She wears a bikini but can surf with the best of them. Although Coco Chanel was the first to make suntans fashionable in the 1940s, it wasn't until the 1960s that the California look began to come together. Hollywood surfers **Gidget** and **Moondoggy** suddenly showed American teens that there were beaches to go to and waves to catch. By the 1970s, as California's population exploded and its homegrown entertainment industry promoted itself, the sun-kissed, blonde-haired, deep-tanned surfer girl was everywhere. Riding in convertibles, skateboarding, or lounging on the beach, she became the American ideal of the 70s.

CALIFORNIA GIRL
IN ACTION

Christie Brinkley in Cover Girl ads (1976–96)

Pamela Anderson, Yasmin Bleeth, and **Traci Bingham** in **TV's Baywatch** (1990–)

Cameron Diaz in **The Sweetest Thing** (2002) and **Charlie's Angels** (2000)

Actor **Heather Locklear**

The TV show **Charlie's Angels** brought athletic California glam to the mainstream small screen. The "angels" were sexy and combative (though ultimately submissive to their mentor Charlie). The standout was golden gal **Farrah Fawcett**, whose incredible shimmering mane flowed behind her as she chased down bad guys. Thousands of teenage girls bought curling brushes and hairspray to imitate that glorious tumble of feathered hair around the face.

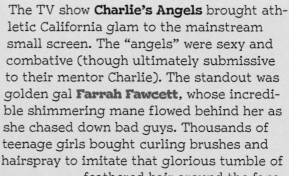
singer beyoncé knowles

The contemporary California Girl isn't necessarily a natural blond from California. **Beyoncé Knowles** of **Destiny's Child** has naturally dark skin, but her blond streaks come from a bottle. In the Shibuya district of Tokyo, Japan, young girls known as **"Ganguro Ko-Gyaru"** bleach their hair and sport dark tans in an ironic take on the California look. **Pamela Anderson** (along with her **Baywatch** buddies) is the California Girl taken to the extreme—her plastic, surgical-balloon take on the look makes her more **Malibu Barbie** (with a touch of porn star) than a real California Girl.

WAVY BLONDE HAIR WITH NATURAL HIGHLIGHTS

NATURAL LOOK: FRECKLES, GLOWY TINTED MOISTURIZER, OR BRONZER

SMILE! PINK LIP GLOSS AND WHITE TEETH

CLASSIC TRIANGLE BIKINI OR SPORTY BIKINI/TANK TOP

EXPOSED MIDRIFF

SHORT SHORTS

SMOOTH, GLOWY SKIN—AND LOTS OF IT SHOWING

TAN, TAN, TAN— (FAKE OR REAL)— AND TAN LINES

CASUAL SHOES, FLIP-FLOPS, SLIDES, OR SNEAKERS WILL WORK.

actor farrah fawcett

Modern beach jocks—swimmers, surfers, beach volleyball players— proudly carry on the natural California Girl tradition, bearing the sun-streaked hair and savage tanned skin. Surfers' hair often gets bleached out at the ends, where it's damaged by sun and sea, creating a signature dark-roots blonde California Girl look.

Golden-brown California Girls have become icons of American culture, of freedom, and (despite that nagging medical evidence about suntans causing cancer) of health. This combo of brown skin and blonde hair evokes perpetual summer and all its kicked-back, sun-warmed implications.

ALSO TRY: SURFER CLOTHES, SPORTY ACCESSORIES LIKE VISORS AND WRISTBANDS

femme fatale

"Femme fatale" is French for "fatal woman"—both the woman all men want to die for and the woman who will lead them to their destruction. The Femme Fatale is the dark side of the Bombshell, the sleek Siamese (with claws) to the Bombshell's fluffy, fun-loving poodle. Her seductive power may not be bowl-you-over obvious, but it's always very powerful—and it always has a price. She may turn on you herself or lead you astray to trouble. Either way, she's dangerous. And that makes her all the more alluring.

actor marlene dietrich

One of the legendary Femme Fatales is **Salome**—as she's represented in literature, anyway. In the original myth, she's a 1st-century Jewish princess whose "Dance of the Seven Veils" so pleases her stepfather, the king, that he offers her anything she wishes as a reward. She asks for the head of John the Baptist in order to carry out her mother's vengeful scheme. It's not until Oscar Wilde's play **Salome** (1893) that Salome's motive becomes sexual. He paints her as a lustful creature driven by anger because she was spurned by John. Artists throughout time have played on the image of an exotic dancer with long, flowing hair and a voluptuous body—evident through her gauzy dress—bewitching the king. Through her seduction, she gets what she wants: destruction.

FEMME FATALE
IN ACTION

Greta Garbo in **Mata Hari** (1932)

Barbara Stanwyck in **Double Indemnity** (1944)

Lana Turner in **The Postman Always Rings Twice** (1946)

Dorothy Dandridge in **Carmen Jones** (1954)

Eartha Kitt in TV's **Batman** (1966–68)

Anne Bancroft in **The Graduate** (1967)

Faye Dunaway in **Chinatown** (1974)

Kathleen Turner in **Body Heat** (1981)

Sharon Stone in **Basic Instinct** (1992)

Linda Fiorentino in **The Last Seduction** (1994)

Sarah Michelle Gellar in **Cruel Intentions** (1999)

julie newmar as catwoman

There are other mythic Femme Fatales. The biblical **Delilah** seduces Samson, who lets her cut his hair and thereby cuts off his strength. In Greek mythology, **Medea** seduces then punishes Jason by slaughtering his children in a monstrous act of revenge.

The Femme Fatale really came into her own, in looks as well as reputation, in the noir films of the 40s. With her ever-so-sensual red lips, she schemed her way through film after film. In classic noirs such as **Double Indemnity** and **The Postman Always Rings Twice**, the Femme Fatale draws one man into a plot designed to rid her of another man. She wants dirty work done, but she doesn't do it herself. Femme Fatales in these and other films often take on a false helplessness or vulnerability as a seduction technique.

Modern Femme Fatales may add new twists to the mix. **Sharon Stone** in **Basic Instinct** is a bisexual seductress. And **Linda Fiorentino** in **The Last Seduction** has capitalist aspirations. Whatever her incarnation, the Femme Fatale is a woman with enduring seductive power—and a willingness to use it to whatever end she sees fit.

SLEEK, SHINY HAIR, SOMETIMES FALLING OVER ONE EYE; DIRTY BLOND, AUBURN, AND CHOCOLATE BROWN ARE CLASSIC FEMME FATALE COLORS.

TRY STRAIGHTENING YOUR HAIR WITH A FLAT IRON FOR MAXIMUM SMOOTHNESS. SHORT HAIR CAN BE SLICKED BACK, AWAY FROM YOUR FACE.

DRAMATIC MAKEUP: SHARPLY DEFINED BROW, SMOKY EYES, AND CONTOURED (NOT BLUSHY) CHEEKS

LONG, VAMPY DARK FINGERNAILS

SLINKY DRESSES IN SATIN OR VELVET; BIAS CUT ENHANCES THE SLINK FACTOR.

FISHNETS OR SEAMED STOCKINGS

STILETTO HEELS

ALSO TRY: GLISTENING BODY LOTION, SLIT SKIRTS OR DRESSES

faerie princess

The faerie princess is one of our more enduring fantasies. Myths and old-time stories feature them—Cinderella's fairy godmother, **A Midsummer Night's Dream's Titania**—hovering about in a gossamer dress, with a wand and an ethereal-yet-full head of hair. The interest of many little girls in becoming ballerinas is connected to the Faerie Princess image: floating through the air with her gauzy tutu, her long hair pinned up to accent the flowing lines of her neck, shoulders, arms.

Fairies aren't all about light—they are magic and magic has a dark side. Fairies use their lightning-quick abilities to pull hair, curdle milk, pinch arms, and generally make miserable anyone who has crossed them.

ophelia **by dagnan-bouveret**

FAERIE PRINCESS
IN ACTION

Subjects in early Renaissance paintings like Sandro Botticelli's **Primavera** (c. 1482)

Women in Pre-Raphaelite paintings like those by Dante Gabriel Rossetti, John Millais, and others (1850s to 1870s)

Musicians/performers **Stevie Nicks, Heart, Melissa auf der Mar** as bass player for **Hole,** and **Tori Amos**

Robin Wright in **The Princess Bride** (1987)

Julia Ormond in **Legends of the Fall** (1994)

Claire Danes in **Romeo and Juliet** (1996)

Cate Blanchett and **Liv Tyler** in **The Fellowship of the Ring** (2001)

Melina Kanakaredes on the TV show **Providence** (2000-)

Many of our images of princesses stem from medieval and Renaissance lore, during the period when fancy dress became a badge of wealth in Europe. (**Faerie** is the medieval spelling in a nod to this influence.) Arthurian legends recount the tale of the lovely **Guinevere** torn between devotion to her husband the king and her growing love for the handsome knight Lancelot. Sandro Botticelli's 15th-century painting **Primavera** (Spring) is a dance of softly curled fair-haired sylphs gently curving beneath diaphanous robes. Delicate pink blooms adorn the flower princess **Flora**, while **Venus**, goddess of love, is wistfully draped in a rich brocade.

FOR MORE ON BOTTICELLI, SEE PAGE 12

Shakespeare's **Ophelia** is an arche-typal Faerie Princess. The daughter of Polonius in **Hamlet**, she's a sweet and virginal young woman eventual-ly driven mad (and suicidal) by love gone wrong. The Victorians, who adored both fairies and tragic love stories, seized upon Ophelia, and Romantic poets and painters have celebrated her ever since. The classic depic-tion is John Millais's **Ophelia** (1851–52).

Stevie Nicks of Fleetwood Mac reclaimed the Faerie Princess from its association with victims and gave it a rocker-girl edge. She says she deliberately chose her look in order to stand out. "I said, 'Instead of going in the direction that a lot of the women singers are going in [revealing] I'll be very, very sexy under 18 pounds of chiffon and lace and velvet...I will have a mystique.'" Nicks succeeded, leaving a rock Faerie Princess legacy that has been adopted by **Heart** and **Tori Amos**. Today's Faerie Princesses bring the romance and magic of fairy tales into the modern age.

singer stevie nicks

ROMANTIC AND ETHEREAL, SHE LOOKS AS IF SHE'D STEPPED OUT OF A FAIRY TALE.

SHIMMERY POWDERS IN PASTELS; LIGHT EYE SHADOW; LONG, FLIRTY LASHES; ROSY CHEEKS

LAYERED HAIR MAY BE LOOSELY TWISTED UP, OR IN RINGLETS; CAN HAVE TWISTED OR BRAIDED PIECES. TRY DELICATE FLOWERED HAIR ACCESSORIES.

SOFT, DEWY LIP GLOSS

ANTIQUE JEWELRY

CORSETS OVER LOOSE, FLOWY CLOTHING

SHEER LAYERS OF FROTHY FABRICS

LACE-UP BOOTS, VICTORIAN STYLE

ALSO TRY: A ROCK-CHICK VERSION OF THE FAERIE PRINCESS BY ADDING BLACK EYELINER AND MORE MAKEUP

island girl

There are as many kinds of Island Girls as there are islands in the world (a lot), but all Island Girls share a love for color and sensuality. She may be inspired by the laid-back vibe of the South Pacific, the Americanized kitsch of Hawaii, or the vibrant energy of the Caribbean...or she may have her own idea of sultry island style. Whether in her natural coastal habitat, or translating the tropics to an urban environment, the Island Girl look is bright, sexy, and fun.

ISLAND GIRL
IN ACTION

Ursula Andress in **Dr. No** (1962)

Bo Derek in **10** (1979)

Tahitian women in **The Bounty** (1984)

Marisa Tomei in **The Perez Family** (1995)

Angela Bassett in **How Stella Got Her Groove Back** (1998)

The Pacific island girl first appeared in the West as the star of luscious paintings by artists such as Paul Gauguin. His solidly built Tahitian women—dressed in simple smocks, sarongs, or nothing at all—were a visual shock to 1890s Paris. Their jet-black hair, often adorned with flowers, streamed down their backs and glistened with coconut oil. A painting like **Tahitian Women** (1891) fills the eye with hot pinks and reds, and sinuous lines.

When Hawaii became an official state in 1959, island culture enjoyed a revival that was at first sincere and has since become kitschy. Plastic leis, fruity umbrella drinks, and loud barkcloth shirts are the tropics viewed through a suburban lens.

a scene from west side story

Tropical Latin-inspired style made waves in North America in the 1940s, when Carmen Miranda brought the bangles and midriffs of the black ghettoes of coastal Brazil to the screen. Halter tops, ruffles, peplums, and flounces are just part of this legacy. In the 1950s, as Puerto Rican emigrés were populating U.S. cities in record numbers, a kind of urban Island Girl style emerged. Body conscious, flirty, and in-your-face sexy, urban island girls went Hollywood in the movie version of **West Side Story** in 1961.

brooke shields in blue lagoon

LONG, SILKY HAIR, ADORNED WITH HIBISCUS OR OTHER TROPICAL, AROMATIC FLOWERS

SHELL JEWELRY

SHIMMERY MAKEUP, GLOSSY LIPS

HALTER TOP OR BIKINI

WELL-OILED SKIN

WAIST AND HIPS ARE OFTEN EXPOSED.

SARONGS IN BOLD COLORS OR TROPICAL PRINTS

ANKLETS

RUFFLES

FEET ARE BARE OR SANDALED; TOE RINGS

The Island Girl look is often more about our idea of the women of the islands than what they really look like. In her more extreme incarnations, she's a kind of fantasy of the torrid tropics, dressed for all-night dance parties (whether she's dancing salsa or hula).

Some Island Girls only appear a few weeks of the year—when on vacation. Then, in the shade of a palm tree, even a buttoned-up lawyer or a grungy tomboy wants to put on a sarong and feel the sand between her toes. The Island Girl gives off a whiff of paradise, which is a nice place to visit, even if very few can call it home.

ALSO TRY: **BELLY CHAINS, FLIMSY BIAS-CUT SLIP DRESSES IN BRIGHT COLORS AND PRINTS**

girl next door

The Girl Next Door generally personifies the mainstream look of her time. She's the "nice girl," the "sweetheart," the opposite of a Femme Fatale. **Mary Pickford**, "America's Sweetheart," was the 1910s and 20s prototype. Cute, cheerful, and always sweet, she became the ideal for the little girl just coming of age. She was the quintessential **Rebecca of Sunnybrook Farm** (1917)—someone you'd like to have in your family or as a friend.

The **Archie** comic series, which started in 1941, illustrated more of the downside to being the sweet supportive type. Girl Next Door Betty did all she could to attract Archie's attention, but he just thought of her as a "friend" while he chased after the more glamorous Veronica. This dynamic reflects a recurring theme of romance novels and movies in which the boy hero is distracted by a glammed-up woman, but in the end realizes that the Girl Next Door is the one for him. (Unfortunately Betty hasn't had her day of reckoning yet.)

GIRL NEXT DOOR
IN ACTION

Mary Pickford in **Pollyanna** (1920)

June Allyson in **Best Foot Forward** (1943) and other 40s musicals

Doris Day in **Pillow Talk** (1959) and other 50s and 60s romantic comedies

Annette Funicello in **Beach Party** (1963) and other 60s beach movies

Meg Ryan in **When Harry Met Sally** (1989)

Julia Roberts in **My Best Friend's Wedding** (1997)

Jennifer Aniston and **Courtney Cox Arquette** in **Friends** (1994–)

In the late 1940s and 50s, it was the peppy, cheerful, cute but not-too-sexy or -glamorous teenagers played by **June Allyson, Jane Powell, Debbie Reynolds,** and **Doris Day** who set the pace on high school and college campuses. They were all innocent and virginal—just the way American girls were supposed to be. With their ponytails or neatly curled poodle cuts, their bobbysox and saddle shoes or kneesocks and penny loafers, they looked all-American clean. In the 1960s the Girl Next Door conquered TV, with **The Patty Duke Show** and **Gidget** (starring **Sally Field**). They were perky and cute, with just a hint of the tomboy.

brandy as TV's moesha

LOW-MAINTENANCE HAIR CAN BE IN A PONYTAIL, PULLED BACK, OR LOOSE (BUT NOT STYLED).

NO-MAKEUP MAKEUP

actor julia roberts

The Girl Next Door can be sporty and tomboyish, tailored and preppy, or girly and sweet. She can wear anything, as long as it doesn't push the style envelope too much. She can also be a girl who is more focused on things other than her look and who wears basics as an antidote to obsessing about fashion.

No matter what, the Girl Next Door exudes wholesomeness. She is, ultimately, a neighbor and her look signifies approachability.

NO NAIL POLISH, OR CLEAR

CASUAL, SIMPLE, AND CLEAN-LOOKING BASICS

SNEAKERS OR BASIC COMFORTABLE SHOES

ALSO TRY: SPORTY LOOKS WITH SWEATS AND OTHER CASUAL ATHLETIC CLOTHES

135

modern primitive

The Modern Primitive is about going back to human roots, to a time when expression was more primal. It taps into a kind of raw power and energy that hasn't been chained down by convention and civilized society.

Fakir Musafar, who coined the term in 1967, says the Modern Primitive is on the hunt for an outer look that expresses the inner spirit. She's a "person who responds to primal urges and does something with the body." Modern Primitive style takes on many of the rituals and visual attributes of ancient and tribal cultures such as piercings and tattoos. These markings make the Modern Primitive identifiable at a glance, but more significantly, they're acquired in a painful ritual that must be felt—to mark significant life experiences with an outward sign.

lucky punk

FOR MORE ON DECORATING THE BODY, SEE PAGES 84–87

MODERN PRIMITIVE
IN ACTION

Betty and Wilma in **The Flintstones** on TV (1960–1966) and film (1994)

Daryl Hannah in **Blade Runner** (1982)

Tina Turner in **Mad Max: Beyond Thunderdome** (1985)

Lori Petty in **Tank Girl** (1995)

Wendy O. Williams of **The Plasmatics**

Ani DiFranco on album **Up Up Up Up Up Up** (1999)

Me'shell N'degeocello on album **Plantation Lullabies** (1993)

Modern Primitives also tend to incorporate clothing and hairstyles that suggest primal times. Hair is often messy and unkempt, sometimes spiky or dreadlocked. Clothing can sometimes reference prehistoric or tribal styles (rough-edged leathers, animal prints) or can be entirely individual, ranging from ripped army fatigues and T-shirts to just about anything ragged and out of the ordinary.

In the late 1970s multiple tattoos, safety-pin piercings, and spiked Mohawk hairstyles in brilliant colors defined punk style, which was a way of rejecting the accepted rules of fashion and "civilization." British designer Vivienne Westwood, who helped fashion the punk look, explained, "The main thing is always to confront the culture...that's what gives you vitality." To find a way to communicate power and authenticity in today's world, Westwood drew inspiration from photographs of tribal peoples. Modern takes on primitive looks became the uniform of the rebel.

SHE'S A RAW, PRIMAL FORCE OF NATURE—A TRIBAL WARRIOR IN THE MODERN WORLD.

UNGROOMED BROWS; ANY MAKEUP (USUALLY JUST EYELINER) IS HAND-SMUDGED.

UNGROOMED HAIR CAN BE SPIKY, CHUNKY, DREAD-LOCKED, OR MOHAWKED. IT SOMETIMES LOOKS DIRTY.

The Modern Primitive look essentially sends a message that says, "I'm part of **my own** culture." With tattoos, piercings, and unkempt hair and clothing, the Modern Primitive is obviously rejecting the clean, mannered rules of fashionable society. She lives by her own rules and wants everyone to know that at a glance.

PIERCINGS

CLOTHING IS NATURAL, IN NEUTRAL COLORS .

LOTS OF HEAVY TRIBAL JEWELRY IN SILVER OR LEATHER

ROUGH-EDGED LEATHER OR SUEDE, REAL-LOOKING FAKE FURS

TATTOOS

HEAVY BOOTS OR CHUNKY SANDALS

at the lollapalooza festival (1991)

ALSO TRY: ANIMAL PRINTS, RIPPED CLOTHING

chic geek

In the 1940s, as men went to war, women went to work—and began wearing suits. At first it was out of necessity. Supplies were scarce and it was easier to retailor a man's suit to fit than to find all the necessary frills for a frock. Working-class women adopted "**Rosie the Riveter**'s" mannish, practical style, and middle- and upper-class women followed the lead of **Lauren Bacall**, wearing sharply tailored suits as they became reporters, administrators, and part of the office landscape.

American women were on their own, fashionwise, for the first time. Until then the American fashion industry had basically followed Paris's lead, but when France was occupied by the Nazis, things changed. The first American sportswear came into being—and it is inextricably tied to the image of a brainy woman making it in a man's world.

CHIC GEEK
IN ACTION

Carole Lombard in **No Man of Her Own** (1932)

"**Brenda Starr, Reporter**" comics from 1941 on

Lois Lane in comics and played by **Margot Kidder** in the **Superman** film series and by **Teri Hatcher** in TV series **Lois and Clark** (1993–97)

Diana Prince/Wonder Woman played by **Lynda Carter** (1976)

Parker Posey in **Party Girl** (1995)

Jodie Foster in **The Silence of the Lambs** (1990)

Velma in **Scooby Doo**, the animated TV series (1969–72) and the film (2002)

In film the professional role that brought the smart/sexy tension to the fore was the "librarian." She wore thick, black-rimmed glasses and sensible suits. But often the meek and properly attired librarian was not all that she seemed to be. Clark Gable couldn't take his eyes off **Carole Lombard**'s legs as she climbed up a ladder to retrieve a book in **No Man of Her Own**. **Katharine Hepburn** is credited most for bringing the smart girl to Hollywood. In **Woman of the Year** (1942) Hepburn was a savvy and sassy world-wise reporter. In **Adam's Rib** (1949) she was a tough-talking lawyer out to win her case. Hepburn's film legacy includes **Party Girl**, where Mary Richards (**Parker Posey**) turned the prim librarian image on its head, bringing the Manhattan club scene into the stacks.

classic geek chic

THIS LOOK CAN BE STRAITLACED OR EDGY DEPENDING ON THE ATTITUDE.

SEVERE HAIR, PULLED BACK OR BOY-CUT SHORT

GLASSES— CAT EYE RETRO OR HEAVY DARK FRAMES

NUDE FACE AND EYE, GROOMED BROWS, RED LIPSTICK FOR AN EDGE

BUTTONED UP— NO SKIN SHOWING

READY-TO-WORK

SUITS OR SWEATERS; CARDIGANS ARE ESPECIALLY CHIC GEEK.

hipster geek chic

The Chic Geek, like the Girl Next Door, is often initially overlooked by the male love interest (at least on TV). Geeks in TV series from **Beverly Hills 90210** to **Buffy the Vampire Slayer** to **Scooby Doo** watch their more glamorous girlfriends get the guy.

But usually the Chic Geek's glasses and prim, tailored clothes mask a smoldering sexuality. Like **Diana Prince** (the female Clark Kent) shedding her sensible suit for her Wonder Woman gear, the Chic Geek knows just when to reveal her powerful, sexual inner self. Modern geek chic is less about seeing smart and sexy as opposing forces and more about synthesizing the two. In the 1990s, riot grrrls wore heavy black glasses with bright red lipstick, driving home the point that girls can be smart, powerful, and sexual all at the same time. With or without the horn rims, smart = sexy, and the Chic Geek knows this better than anyone.

LADYLIKE PENCIL SKIRT, OR PANTS (COULD BE MEN'S TOO, FOR A BOXIER LOOK)

OPAQUE TIGHTS (TRY PATTERNED ONES FOR SOME FUN)

PUMPS, SLINGBACKS, OR CLUNKY MEN'S OXFORDS

ALSO TRY: VINTAGE SWEATERS OR SUITS, MEN'S UNIFORM PANTS, ARGYLES OR STRIPES

showgirl

The Showgirl is what the name says: a girl on show. All the world's a stage for the Showgirl, and she lives to perform for the spotlight and the audience. The Showgirl is flamboyant, exuberant, more out there than the Bombshell and way more over-the-top than the Diva. No fashion statement is too outrageous—beads, feathers, curls, spangles are just the beginning.

The Showgirl has a long and varied history, and many incarnations. Vegas showgirls, burlesque queens, geishas, flamenco dancers—even belly dancers—are all Showgirls, and they all share one thing: the need to have all eyes on them.

cher in bob mackie

SHOWGIRL
IN ACTION

Women in **Busby Berkeley** films like **42nd Street** (1933)

Burlesque stars **Gypsy Rose Lee, Lili St. Cyr** and **Blaze Starr**

Judy Garland in **Ziegfeld Girl** (1941)

Barbra Streisand as **Fanny Brice** in **Funny Girl** (1968)

Liza Minnelli in **Cabaret** (1972)

Bette Midler in **Divine Madness!** (1980)

Apollonia in **Purple Rain** (1984)

Lolita Davidovich in **Blaze** (1989)

performer josephine baker

Some of the most famous Showgirls of modern times were the high-stepping **Can-can girls** of 1830s **Paris**, immortalized by artist Henri de Toulouse-Lautrec. The first American Showgirls appeared in traveling vaudeville shows from about 1880 to 1930. Typical vaudeville shows had skits, magic, comedy, and singing, and Showgirls were expected to be versatile and eyecatchingly glamorous.

The prototypical Showgirls were the **Ziegfeld Girls** of the famous vaudeville **Ziegfeld Follies**. A Ziegfeld girl glided across the stage, smiling and moving like a swan. You'd never know from looking at her that the feathered headdress weighed ten pounds, her dangerously high heels were killing her, or that her sequined brief was giving her a wedgie. The Showgirl knows that the show must go on at all costs.

WHEN YOU'RE A SHOWGIRL, ALL THE WORLD'S A STAGE.

BIG HAIR IS A MAJOR SHOWGIRL LOOK. SHOWGIRLS ALSO LIKE BRIGHT HAIR COLORS AND CRAZY TEXTURES.

Life is a cabaret, but most Showgirls go off-stage eventually. You can't be a Showgirl 24/7—unless you want your whole life to be a performance. Every theater has a back-stage, and generally Showgirls have other lives in which their flair for drama is less visible.

MAKEUP IS BRIGHT, GLITTERY, SHINY, SHOWY. THE SHOWGIRL DOES NOT GO FOR THE NATURAL LOOK.

BOAS WERE MADE FOR SHOWGIRLS.

Today's Showgirls encompass a wide variety of entertainment, both mainstream and fringe, often incorporating his-toric and international Showgirl styles. Exotic dancers, drag queens, and pop stars all work the look. A Showgirl isn't worried about "being taken seriously." She wants to wear costumes that sometimes shock, sometimes amuse, but always get her noticed—whether she's onstage or at a party.

LOTS OF SKIN

FASHIONWISE, THERE IS NO SUCH THING AS "TOO MUCH." SEQUINS, FEATHERS, SATIN, LEATHER, FAKE FUR, SEE-THROUGH, SKIMPY, SPARK-LY, SHINY, TIGHT, BRIGHT, AND JUST PLAIN KOOKY ARE ALL FAIR GAME, EVEN AT THE SAME TIME. IT JUST DEPENDS ON WHAT KIND OF SHOW-GIRL YOU WANT TO BE.

PLATFORM SHOES AND OTHER HEELS MAKE THE SHOWGIRL LARGER THAN LIFE.

SEE THE NEXT PAGE FOR SOME DIFFERENT KINDS OF SHOWGIRL LOOKS FROM HISTORY AND AROUND THE WORLD.

ALSO TRY: ANYTHING ATTENTION-GETTING!

LAS VEGAS SHOWGIRL

The Las Vegas Showgirl was first introduced to America in the 1940s. The costumes she wore were as outlandish as they were spectacular, with exotic fabrics barely covering her body. Large fans and feathers sprouting out from the costume could make her seem eight feet tall and six feet wide. The headdress, her crowning feature, was decorated with sequins, rhinestones, and all things glitzy. As the Las Vegas spectacular has evolved to involve more movement and dance, the once lavish costumes have given way to simpler, lighter outfits.

FLAMENCO

The origins of flamenco can be traced back to 16th-century Spain and are rooted in Gypsy history. The most recognizable visual aspect of flamenco is the costume worn by the dancers. The brightly colored dress looks almost like a guitar with its low neck, tight waist, and wide hips. The frills on the bottom half of the dress swish to dramatic effect as the dancer struts around the stage, emphasizing her footwork (she wears special shoes to tap out the rhythms) as well as her flirtatious relationship with the audience. The dancer usually wears her hair away from her face to accentuate her neck.

flamenco dancer

BURLESQUE

Vaudeville morphed into burlesque (derived from the Italian "burlescho," meaning "mockery") in the early 1900s, with a new, bolder sexual innuendo. By the 1920s the sexual nature became so pervasive that women stopped attending performances. Burlesque was redefined as a showplace for provocatively clad women. After striptease was introduced as an element of the burlesque in New York City in the 1920s, striptease "artistes" like **Gypsy Rose Lee**, **Lili St. Cyr**, and **Blaze Starr** became burlesque stars. The look was overtly sexual, with feather boas, strategically placed sequins, and bikini-style outfits (which were often removed to reveal even more).

gypsy rose lee

BELLY DANCERS

The belly dance, also known as "Raks Sharki" or dance of the East, is an ancient Middle Eastern custom that dates back to pagan times. Originally the dance was a sacred ceremony honoring the mysteries of childbirth—and was meant to be seen by women only. Paying homage to the goddesses, a single dancer moved her hips, chest, and stomach. Over time, belly dancing evolved into a spectacle, with dancers performing for men in nightclub-style environments. The costumes of the dancers consequently became more revealing. Thus the image of a shiny bra, low-riding pants, and bejeweled belly button that we typically associate with the belly dancer are a far cry from the loose tunics that Middle Eastern women originally wore. Scarves, chains, and metallic clothes and accessories also evolved from the sexualized belly-dancer look.

belly dancer

GEISHAS

The geisha has a long and distinct tradition in Japan. "Gei" means accomplishment or performance and "sha" means person. The geishas were people (originally men, then women) who were accomplished in the performing and social arts. Their skills were used to entertain and relax men at formal parties and events.

Today, geisha is a very dignified and respected profession. A geisha must undergo years of training in which she learns the many intricacies of traditional Japanese music and dance. The appearance of a geisha is also very specific and distinct. Her hair is held up with a number of hairpins and is styled to look like the leaf of a ginkgo tree. Her face is painted white and her lips highlighted in red. A geisha will wear an expensive floral kimono made of silk and tied at the waist with a silk obi. The elaborate ensemble obliterates the curves of the body. Attention is then turned to the hands, face, and especially the neck, which is exposed by the geisha's upswept hairdo.

geisha

more style sources

cultural pride

Many communities use style as a way to display pride in their cultural heritage, particularly in the culturally diverse United States. Certain kinds of fashion can show a commitment to retaining and celebrating the visual heritage of the group you identify with—or want to be identified with. Wearing clothing that identifies you culturally can be a way of saying "I haven't forgotten where I came from." It can be particularly necessary for individuals who must negotiate the difference between the dominant culture and their own smaller one. A black girl who attends an all-white school and accessorizes her uniform with a head scarf in African colors is telling both communities that she takes her roots with her wherever she goes. These kind of looks can be subtle or full-on, anything from wearing a full Salwar kameez (the Indian fashion of a long tunic over pants) to simply adding a bindi to an otherwise western outfit.

FOR MORE ON HOW TRADITIONS AND BELIEFS SHAPE THE WAY PEOPLE DRESS, SEE PAGE 24

street style

The idea of street style is that it's real life fashion—what people wear in the real world, not on a runway or in a magazine.

"The street" can be literal—in cities, the street is where style is on parade—or it can be a metaphor for wherever people hang out and strut their stuff. Whatever the location, street style is an expression of the distinctive creativity of young people and the unique sensibilities of the environments they live in.

These looks may start in particular neighborhoods but get picked up by larger society. The tough look of East LA Latina girls, with strong lip liner, low slung pants, and heavily sprayed hair can be seen in Midwest malls and even overseas. Street styles often arise in connection with subcultures, as in the case of 1970s London punk, 80s inner-city hip-hop, and the Seattle "grunge" look (flannel shirts, wool knit caps, and biker boots with dresses), all of which have made their presence felt on designer catwalks. And the cool graphics and relaxed-yet-edgy style of skateboard culture have influenced a generation of everyday fashion.

An individual on the street (whether it's the neohippie Portabello Road in London, trendy Harajuku in Tokyo, or Your Town, USA) is presenting a distillation of his or her personality. To an outsider, everyone in a certain neighborhood may look the same; but if you live there, you know the nuance of every little thing. Some communities think it's cool when their look gets picked up by the mainstream, but others want to keep their street style to themselves—so they have to keep changing it.

music

Music means a lot to people, often expressing a particular attitude or outlook on life. Musical subcultures arise when people identify with this attitude and a corresponding style emerges that is reflective of it. Sometimes fans study musicians and copy their look, within certain budgetary and functionality limits (travelling everywhere in a limo has its advantages). But the fashion doesn't just flow from the top down—lots of musical subcultures have produced their own mini-archetypes. Everyone knows a Grateful Dead fan by her tie-dye!

HIP HOP

The hip hop girl's look is a blend of high fashion, cultural pride, and street style. It has its roots in the inner-city, where "B-boy" hip hop pioneers sported cool attitudes that matched their defiant lyrics. They wore baggy pants with a swathe of underwear showing above the low-slung waist. Nowadays, B-girls (and boys) are more likely to show off rock hard abs instead. They may wear their hair in braids or cornrows—or incorporate preppy components into their look with all-American sportswear like baseball jerseys and caps worn purposely oversize or askew. Hip-hop style often has a "bling bling" showiness to it, expressed with over-the-top designer clothes and logos, and flashy jewelry. Gold chains and big rings (a part of hip hop culture dating back to the B-boys) reflect the good old American obsession with wealth and status, but can also mockingly refer to stereotypes of African American pimps and drug dealers.

HIP HOP

da brat

RAVE

Rave culture at its most idealistic is about a youthful, good-vibe globalism and its fashion reflects that. A rave girl wears comfortable, often childlike clothes. So-called "candy ravers" take this look the furthest, adding elements from children's books like Dr. Seuss hats or jewelry made from toys, even pacifier necklaces, to their pajama-like outfits. (The pajamas come in handy at all-night parties). This happy-go-lucky look actually derives from the outfits ecstasy dealers used to wear to identify themselves. The rave girl wants to bring her benevolent fantasy to life and loves to add glitter, angel wings, or other accessories to her outfit. She may wear absorbent clothes and tiny tops—in case she works up a sweat dancing.

RAVE

PUNK

The punk rock scene took off around 1977. New York City was the first hotbed of punk music, but London was the center of punk fashion. Malcolm McClaren (who managed the Sex Pistols) and designer Vivienne Westwood generated punk trends from their radical style shops. The old school punks rejected acceptable society and dressed accordingly with spiky hair, ripped clothes, and metal chains. They further adorned/uglified themselves by sticking safety pins through their cheeks and lips. Conservative society was horrified but the kids loved it. Today's punks, sometimes called "hardcore," dress similarly, but don't cause quite as big a stir. When mainstream pop stars have pink hair and suburban housewives wear studded leather, punk's shocking roots seem quaint.

OTHER MUSIC

Country and western music celebrates American independence and self-reliance by incorporating the boots and hats of the frontier. Recently Madonna took a

PUNK

country look out of the grand ole opry and onto MTV. "Indie" music scenesters, rebelling against the 1980s and 90s extravagant displays of wealth, went thrifting for more low-key fashions with a vintage vibe. Indieboys or girls sometimes favor a mod gas station attendant look in work pants, a windbreaker, and a T-shirt or button-down shirt. Cardigans, retro dresses with clunky shoes, and chunky glasses are also part of the Indie look.

FREEDOM of style

possibilities and options

The looks in this section are what we call "archetypes," which means they represent a certain ideal of beauty from which other looks are derived. But for every ideal we present in this book, there are ten more that you don't see here. And beyond these archetypes and others, there's a wide world of incarnations and combinations of looks for you to explore.

You may page through this book and find one look that makes you think, "Hey, that's MY look." Or you may find the look that's been sitting around inside you twiddling its thumbs waiting for the opportunity to be discovered and see the light of day (or night). Or you may see ten different looks that you find vaguely interesting, and nothing that particularly speaks to your sense of style. You may have always had a burning desire to look like Marilyn Monroe, or James Dean. Or you may not have thought much at all about looking like anybody but YOU. In any case, you've got a multitude of options and resources to work with.

There's no need to follow the looks in this book to the letter. Style is a personal thing, and it's what you bring to a look—your face, your body, and, most important, your personality—that makes it yours. If a head-to-toe makeover is more than you're in the mood for, you can experiment with looks on a much smaller scale. Something as simple as lipstick color can impact the way you look and feel. Dark lipstick can make you feel Goth, pale lipstick can make you feel Mod. Shoes, hair, and jewelry can all have the same kind of effect. The important thing is how you feel about how you look. If you walk around feeling like an old-school movie star or a secret vampire, a little of that sense of style is likely to rub off on the people who see you.

combinations and creations

Whether it's on the screen or the street, many people choose to mix and match styles to find their own image of beauty. Unique style comes from being creative and playing with the possibilities...creating an archetype of your own.

Innovative fashion icons develop inventive combos of style that define their own beauty ideals. Other stylemakers work their way through the rounds of ideal beauties, putting their own personal touch on each one. This emphasizes the power of style as a kind of play, and not something that needs to seriously define who you are.

Most famously, Madonna has been a Bad Girl, Bombshell, Showgirl, Bohemian, Androgyne, Femme Fatale, Vamp/Goth, Diva, and more. And while the image of her in each of these guises is part of our idea of

MADONNA'S MANY LOOKS

bombshell

androgyne

power jock

showgirl

Madonna-ness, her chameleon-like persona makes it clear that the "real" Madonna is the person who lives beneath the fashion, not any individual look.

expression!

Your style is not your self. But it is a way for you to express yourself and your ideas (and anything else you think is interesting). And it is a very powerful form of expression. By taking the power of style into your own hands, you can transform your image, turning yourself into a Bombshell or a Bad Girl or a Boy/girl for a day (or every day). You can use a look to express to the world who you truly feel you are, or play with looks to show that you're more than an image.

Style is so much more than what's "in style" this minute. It's a way of communicating—and a way of showing yourself off to the world for your entire life.

Have fun with it!

debbie harry

It can be fun to analyze people's style and try to figure out what inspires their looks. Lots of images of beauty and style refer to an archetype or two...

mod/new wave

bettie page

resources

Check out our first book, **DEAL WITH IT! A Whole New Approach to Your Body, Brain, and Life as a gURL**. It's a great resource for almost anything a young woman might encounter en route to adulthood—what you need to know about safe sex, pregnancy, self-destructive behavior, and so much more.

For web sites, organizations, hard-to-find books, and updated resources relevant to this book, see www.thelooksbook.com.

Let us know if you have any suggestions!

Here's an incomplete list of books that might be useful or interesting to you.

BEAUTY

The Art of Makeup by Kevyn Aucoin (HarperCollins, 1996).
Beauty tips and instruction from one of Hollywood's favorite makeup artists.

Asian Beauty by Margaret Kimura, Marianne Dougherty, Rich Marchewka (Harper Resource, 2001)
Makeup artist Kimura's guide to makeup techniques specifically for Asian women.

Beauty: The New Basics by Rona Berg (Workman Publishing Company, 2001)
Step-by-step makeovers with head-to-toe beauty tips.

The Beauty Myth by Naomi Wolf (Anchor, 1992)
Describes how cultural messages about female beauty help to oppress women.

Beyond Beauty by Jane Pratt (Clarkson Potter, 1997)
A collection of photos with profiles of teenagers, exploring their views on beauty and fashion, among other things.

Bodies of Subversion: A Secret History of Women and Tattoo by Margot Mifflin (Power House Cultural Entertainment, 2001)
An illustrated cultural history of the art of tattoo.

Curly Girl by Lorraine Massey and Deborah Chiel (Workman Publishing Company, 2001)
Care and styling for women with curls.

Don't Go to the Cosmetics Counter Without Me by Paula Begoun (Beginning Press, 2000)
Surprising and sometimes frightening consumer information on common hazardous ingredients in thousands of branded beauty products.

Earthly Bodies, Heavenly Hair by Dina Falconi (Ceres Press, 1997)
Info and recipes for do-it-yourself natural cosmetics and body care.

Face Forward by Kevyn Aucoin (Little Brown & Company, 2000)
A forward-thinking book of makeovers featuring both familiar and unfamiliar faces.

Fine Beauty: Beauty Basics and Beyond for African-American Women by Sam Fine and Julia Chance (Riverhead Books, 1999)
A lavish beauty book, specifically geared towards African American women.

Hope In A Jar: The Making of America's Beauty Culture by Kathy Lee Peiss (Owl Books, 1999)
A cultural history of the American beauty business.

Latina Beauty by the Editors of Latina Magazine and Belen Aranda-Alvarado (Hyperion, 2000)
A guide for Hispanic women.

Lipstick by Jessica Pallingston (St. Martins Press, 1999)
A fun, fact-filled look at the history of our most popular cosmetic.

Making Faces by Kevyn Aucoin (Little Brown & Company, 1999)
A book that brilliantly shows the power of transformation through style.

Makeup Your Mind by Francois Nars (powerHouse Books, 2002)
A beautiful, extremely useful book about face makeup, from the creator of the Nars line.

Modern Primitives by V. Vale (Re-Search Publications, 1989)
The classic, illustrated exploration of ancient human decoration practices such as tattooing, piercing, and scarification.

Natural Body Basics: Making Your Own Cosmetics by Dorie Byers (Gooseberry Hill Publications, 1996)
An introduction to homemade cosmetics.

No Lye! The African-American Woman's Guide to Natural Hair Care by Tulani Kinard (St. Martin's Press, 1997)
A leading black stylist's guide to great-looking hair without chemicals.

The Quest for Human Beauty: An Illustrated History by Julian Robinson (WW Norton & Company, 1998)
A fascinating investigation of how people in different places and times have pursued beauty.

Real Gorgeous: The Truth About Body and Beauty by Kaz Cooke (WW Norton & Company, 1996)
A humorous and empowering look at the forces that shape our body and beauty images.

Survival of the Prettiest by Nancy Etcoff (Anchor Books, 2000)
A scientific exploration of beauty.

Ultimate Makeup and Beauty by Mary Quant (DK Publishing, 1996).
A definitive guide to selecting products and using them, from a woman who knows what she's talking about.

Venus Envy by Elizabeth Haiken (Johns Hopkins University Press, 1999)
The evolution of cosmetic surgery over the last hundred years.

Your Makeover: Simple Ways for Any Woman to Look Her Best by Morgen Schick DeMann (Universe, May 2000)
Tips and tricks from a pro for easy beauty.

FASHION & STYLE

Audrey Style by Pamela Clarke Keogh (HarperCollins, 1999)
Audrey Hepburn, the fashion icon and the person.

The Bombshell Manual of Style by Laren Stover (Hyperion, 2001)
A how-to book for wanna-be bombshells.

China Chic: East Meets West by Valerie Steele (Yale University Press, 1999)
How Chinese fashion has influenced Western fashion, and vice-versa.

Corsets and Crinolines by Norah Waugh (Routledge/Theatre Arts Books, 1991)
A history of old-school undergarments.

The Corset: A Cultural History by Valerie Steele (Yale University Press, 2001)
An intellectual reading of the meaning of corsets.

Extreme Beauty: The Body Transformed by Harold Koda (Metropolitan Museum of Art, 2001)
An interesting visual review of the various ways the body and silhouette have been shaped through history and in fashion.

Fashion a la Mode by Isabelle de Borchgrave (Universe 2000)
Beautifully painted and crafted pop-up installations of important fashion eras.

The Fashion Book by Phaidon Press (2001)
Lavishly illustrated encyclopedia of fashion.

Fashion Through the Ages: From Overcoats to Petticoats by Margaret Knight (Viking, 1998)
A simple illustrated fashion history with cute lift-up flaps so you can see what's underneath the outerwear.

Fast, Fun Fashion: 101 Ways to Customize Your Clothes by Petra Boase (Carlton, 2001)
Easy ways to make your clothes your own.

Fifty years of Fashion by Valerie Steele (Yale University Press, 2000)
A photographic survey of modern fashion from the New Look to now.

The Fine Art of Dressing: Make Yourself a Masterpiece by Dressing for Your Body Type by Margaux Tartarotti (Perigee, 1999)
Fashion ideas for different body types based on the ideals of painters like Modigliani, Rubens, Gauguin and others.

Fruits by Shoichi Aoki (Phaidon, 2001)
Young people of Tokyo show off their supremely creative street style.

Jackie: The Clothes of Camelot by Jay Mulvaney (St. Martin's Press, 2001)
A survey of the fashionable first lady's looks.

The Language of Clothes by Alison Lurie (Owl Books, 2000)
A classic book about what we wear—and what it says about who we are

The Power of Style:The Women Who Defined the Art of Living Well by Annette Tapert and Diana Edkins (Crown, 1994)
Profiles of Coco Chanel, Diana Vreeland, and other stylish ladies.

The Rudi Gernreich Book by Peggy Moffit and Marylou Luther (Taschen, 1999)
Mr. Mod, by the model he made famous.

20,000 Years of Fashion: The History of Costume & Personal Adornment by Francois Leon Louis Boucher (Harry N. Abrams, 1987)
A big, fat fashion reference.

ART, MEDIA, AND CULTURE

The Evolution of Allure by George Hersey (MIT Press, 1996)
A high-falutin' romp through the overlap of art history and biology.

From Mae to Madonna: Women Entertainers in Twentieth-Century America by June Sochen (University Press of Kentucky, 1999)
The impact of women in entertainment and their effect on American culture.

From Reverence to Rape: The Treatment of Women in the Movies by Molly Haskell (University of Chicago Press, 1987)
A look at how women have been treated on film throughout the 20th century.

Mammies No More: The Changing Image of Black Women on Stage and Screen by Lisa M. Anderson (Rowman & Littlefield, 1997)
Explores how stereotypes of black women have been reflected and reinforced in the theatre and cinema.

The Nude by Kenneth Clark (Princeton University Press, 1972)
Classic historical analysis of nudes in art, and what they mean.

She's A Rebel: The History of Women in Rock & Roll by Gillian G. Gaar (Seal Press, 2002).

Explores the role of rock and pop heroines.

20th Century Rock and Roll: Women in Rock by Dale Sherman (Collector's Guide Publications, 2001)
Profiles of 50 influential musicians and icons.

Understanding Comics by Scott McCloud (Kitchen Sink Press, 1994)
A comic book that can change the way you think about media.

Ways of Seeing by John Berger (Viking, 1995)
Accessible, groundbreaking work about media, culture and perception.

We Gotta Get Out of This Place by Gerri Hirshey (Atlantic Monthly Press, 2001)
One woman's history of women in rock 'n' roll.

We're Desperate: the Punk Rock Photography of Jim Jocoy (PowerHouse Books, 2002)
Punk style captured on film, with writing from music and fashion icons.

Where the Girls Are: Growing up Female with the Mass Media by Susan J. Douglas (Random House, 1995)
An exploration of the representation of American women in postwar American media.

TAKING CARE OF YOUR BODY

Ayurveda for Women by Dr. Robert E. Svoboda (Inner Traditions, 2000)
A guide to vitality for every stage of a woman's life, based on this ancient Indian system.

The Body Project: An Intimate History of American Girls by Joan Jacobs Brumberg (Vintage Books, 1998)
A historical look at how American girls' bodies and body images have changed during the last two centuries.

Eating Well for Optimum Health by Dr. Andrew Weil (Quill, 2001)
A solid guide to healthy eating that simplifies confusing and conflicting nutritional information.

Fat Talk: What Girls and Their Parents Say about Dieting by Mimi Nichter (Harvard University Press, 2000)
Based on a three-year study of teen-aged girls, an anthropological study of the forces that influence girls' self-image.

The Fitness Factor by Dr. Lisa Callahan (Lyons Press, 2002)
A sports medicine specialist details the connection between exercise and health, with practical advice for working fitness into your life.

Food and Mood by Elizabeth Somer (Owl Books, 1999)
How nutrients in food can affect the way you feel, think and behave.

The Go Ask Alice Book of Answers: A Guide to Good Physical, Sexual and Emotional Health by Columbia University's Health Education Program (Owl Books, 1998)
Gives straightforward, honest answers to teenagers' questions.

The Heart of Yoga: Developing a Personal Practice by T.K.V. Desikachar (Inner Traditions, 1998)
The practice of yoga directed toward people's individual needs.

Light on Yoga by B. K. S. Iyenger (Schocken, 1995)
A definitive guide to the philosophy and practice of yoga.

A Woman's Book of Strength by Karen Andes, (Perigee Books, 1995)
An inspiring, empowering, and practical guide to mind-body fitness.

Women's Bodies, Women's Wisdom by Christiane Northrup (Bantam Doubleday Dell, 1998)
A holistic approach to physical and emotional health and healing.

NOT TAKING CARE OF YOUR BODY

EATING DISORDERS

The Eating Disorder Sourcebook by Carolyn Costin (McGraw Hill, 1999)
A fairly comprehensive guide to the causes, treatments, and prevention of a range of eating disorders.

Hunger Pains: The Modern Woman's Tragic Quest for Thinness by Mary Pipher, Ph.D. (Ballantine Books, 1997)
Looks at cultural causes of eating disorders, and encourages girls and women to accept their bodies.

SELF-MUTILATION

Bodily Harm by Karen Conterio and Wendy Lader with Jennifer Kingson Bloom (Hyperion, 1999)
Defines self-injury and the reasons behind it.

Cutting: Understanding & Overcoming Self-Mutilation by Steven Levenkron (WW Norton & Co., 1999)
Explains what causes the disorder and how to help the self-mutilator.

Help for Hair Pullers: Understanding and Coping with Trichotillomania by Nancy Keuthen, Gary Christenson and Dan Stein (New Harbinger Pub, 2001)
Describes the treatment options for controlling trichotillomania.

Obsessive Compulsive Disorders: Getting Well and Staying Well by Fred Penzel (Oxford University Press, 2000)
Gives advice on helping trichotillomania, OCD, skin-picking and nail-biting.

Women Who Hurt Themselves: A Book of Hope and Understanding by Dusty Miller (Basic Books, 1995)
Looks at the roots of self-inflicted injury in women.

photo credits

index